01-17-08

W9-AEO-368

Peanut Soup and Spoonbread:

An Informal History of Hotel Roanoke

By Donlan Piedmont

Authorized by Virginia Tech Real Estate Foundation, Inc.,

COPYRIGHT ©1994 VIRGINIA TECH REAL ESTATE FOUNDATION, INC.

ALL RIGHTS RESERVED. NO PORTION OF THIS BOOK CAN BE REPRODUCED WITHOUT
WRITTEN PERMISSION OF THE VIRGINIA TECH REAL ESTATE FOUNDATION, INC.

LIBRARY OF CONGRESS CATALOG CARD NUMBER 94-44863

ISBN 0-9617635-1-5

FIRST PRINTING: NOVEMBER 1994

ALL CREDITS OF THE PHOTOGRAPHS AND ARTWORK IN THIS BOOK
ARE REFERENCED AS TO SOURCE IN THE PHOTOGRAPH APPENDIX

PUBLISHED BY THE VIRGINIA TECH REAL ESTATE FOUNDATION, INC.

PRINTED IN ROANOKE, VIRGINIA BY PROGRESS PRESS,INC.

To Hotel Roanoke,
its people, its past and its future,

and

to Dot

this book is dedicated –
with affection for the first
and love for the second

"The place with that lovely hotel."

During an airborne mission behind enemy lines in New Guinea in the Second World War, Bill Gearhart, Roanoker, and his commander, a lieutenant-colonel in the Australian Army, took advantage of a rare idle moment.

"Well, leftenant," the Australian asked, "where in the States do you come from?"

"Virginia, sir."

"I have been in Virginia. What city?"

"Roanoke, sir."

"Ah, Roanoke, the place with that lovely hotel."

"The place with that lovely hotel" ...invoked in a steamy green hell thousands of miles from the recalled elegance and charm of the Roanoke landmark.

Carter Burgess, distinguished citizen, once said that he was one of those Roanokers "who had never been south of Winston-Salem or north of New York until the war. I've been all over the world many times since then, and just about everywhere I went, I heard something about Hotel Roanoke from people who had wonderful memories of the place."

Such was the nature of the far-flung reputation of Roanoke's "Grand Old Lady on the Hill," a place which, from its beginnings in 1882, was the locus of the city's social and cultural life. The city and the Hotel, virtually founded together, were bound up in an indefinable almost mystical symbiosis, each drawing nourishment and growth from the other. The Hotel brought visitors to the city—famous and otherwise, such disparate personalities as Nelson Rockefeller and Billy Sunday, J. P. Morgan and William Jennings Bryan, Richard Nixon and Alben Barkley, Amelia Earheart and Van Cliburn—and gave employment to generations of Roanoke citizens, most of them black. (It is a cruel and poignant fact of history that the Hotel had been flourishing for 82 years before blacks could come into it through the front door instead of the employee entrance, and order dinner instead of serve it.)

It was a part of Roanoke's life, the Hotel was, and mine too. My first date with Dorathy Brown was in its Fountain Room of happy memory. Less than a year later, we were in the Pine Room for our wedding reception. Marie and Richard Dunlap and Libbe and William Hubard and Sara and Jack Airheart, all Roanokers, spent part of their honeymoons there (one night costing the Airhearts $10.00 plus a 50-cent tax and a $3.00 restaurant charge). Catherine Blair Fisher remembers that it was in the Regency Room that she had her first champagne cocktail. There were weddings, christenings and even a funeral, when the ashes of a frequent and long-staying guest were scattered on the grounds. There were dances, parties, conventions, and the Hotel moved to a national and even, as we have seen, an international reputation.

It produced Chef Fred Brown's peanut soup, Ken Wilkey's Whistle Stop, Fred Walker's and Carl Thurston's Virginia Night, Peter Kipp's Ad Lib Club, Janet Jenkin's 30-year career of steady devotion, Doreen Hamilton Fishwick's valedictory, and for all who even once passed through its corridors, fond memories and nostalgia in bulk.

The Hotel was sustained by its railroad owner through the storms and calms of a hundred years; funds were always forthcoming, perhaps reluctantly but always generously and sometimes bravely, as when it made a significant investment for a major expansion in the Depression year of 1931. It became a corporate jewel to be polished and admired; it was a "club without dues," said one patron, "a club without membership," according to another. It was a place for lunch, a place for a drink, a place to meet friends, a place to make deals, smooth paths, settle civic matters. It dominated the city as socially as it did topographically, with its view of downtown just across the railroad tracks from its little hill.

The Hotel enjoyed a generally sunny passage through its 107 years, though dark clouds did occasionally cast shadows over it. A principal one was the employee strike which began at dinner on the night of October 1, 1983 and ended six months later in April 1984. The issue was wages and working conditions. Management, facing a competitive crunch, sought ways to reduce full-time employment and keep wage increases to a minimum. Called at home when the walkout took place, Peter Kipp and his wife went immediately to the Regency Room. With other management personnel the Kipps waited on the tables, demonstrating in an odd sort of way the Hotel's unwavering commitment to service. Replacements were hired, and a large meeting scheduled two days later was handled without incident.

My aim in writing this work is not to produce the definitive history of Hotel Roanoke, but to try to define and parse its

reputation and character; hoping at least to suggest its rich tradition, its warmth, its people and the affectionate hold it exerted on so many, an affection that has continued even beyond the day it closed, November 30, 1989. I have learned that those who worked there, those who stayed there, and those who perhaps only passed it by all looked on it with awe, affection, joy, disappointment and sadness, the whole range of human experience. I accept the burden of all of this book's flaws and omissions; but if, after reading it, people who have known the Hotel can say, "Yes, that's the way it was;" or "I remember that!" and those who have never set foot inside the place can say, "What a wonderful place it must have been!" then I am more than willing to declare myself satisfied.

Deserving a large measure of whatever success that may attach to this effort, but totally exempt from its failures, are many, many people who gave their time and wisdom with kindness and patience. I cannot assign priorities of gratitude, but I am especially indebted to Janet Jenkins, retired general manager (described by several different persons as "a great lady") for her memories and insights of the place that meant so much to her, and to three other former general managers of Hotel Roanoke—Doreen Hamilton Fishwick (its last), Peter Kipp and Fred Walker, who have been to me generosity personified. Thanks too to these former Hotel employees: Vickie Stump Cutting, Bruce Coffey, Lynn Schumacher, Mark Lambert, "Billy" Davis, Alphonso "Alex" Alexander, Warren Webb and Heinz Schlagel. My thanks go as well to Clare White, a historian of formidable talent and broad knowledge of the early days of Roanoke, and Dr. Nancy Connelly, executive director, both of the Roanoke Valley History Museum; to the staff of the Special Collections at the Carol Newman Library at Virginia Tech,

Dorothy and Donlan Piedmont's wedding reception; Pine Room, 1954

especially Laura Katz Smith, to Belinda Harris of the library of the *Roanoke Times & World News*, to Carol Tuckwiller of the Virginia Room of the Roanoke City Public Library and to Ken Miller.

Providing both information and insights from Norfolk and Western Railway and Norfolk Southern Corporation were John P. Fishwick, who was called from retirement by the late chairman of Norfolk Southern, Robert Claytor, to oversee Hotel operations, and who with Arnold B. McKinnon presided over its donation to the Virginia Tech Foundation; Richard F. Dunlap, Lawrence Forbes, William B. Bales, Reggie Short, Larry Keoughan, Arnold McKinnon, John Turbyfill, Richard Parker, Don Middleton, George Ruff , Frank Wilner, later a vice president of the Association of American Railroads, and Ann Fox Sprague, one time assistant editor of the *Norfolk and Western Magazine*. Invaluable too were Roanoke City Manager Bob Herbert, retired banker Dave Caudill and Virginia Tech's vice president Minnis Ridenour who, with John Fishwick, supplied facts and background to the long and complex negotiations which culminated in the offer of the Hotel to Virginia Tech and its acceptance and the agreement of the City to build a conference center in connection with the Hotel.

Among individuals who helped me in one way or another are, in no particular order, Carter Burgess, Michael Ramsey, Senator John Warner, Senator Charles Robb, former Congressman James Olin, Robert Garland, Ray Garland, Austin Neal, Kitty Fisher, John Vaughan, Margaret Baker, Elizabeth Bowles, William McClung, Charles Lunsford, Helen Fitzpatrick, Henry Hewitt, Betty Carr Muse, Mona Black, Ann Hammersley, John Eure and Sara and Jack Airheart, and many, many more. They gave substance to this work and encouragement to its author by a word, a reference, a memory or two. I tender special thanks to Michael Ramsey and to Bill McClung (retired Public Affairs Director of Appalachian Power Company, and an old boss of mine), who were both kind enough to read portions of the manuscript and offer constructive comments and suggestions, some of which I accepted. Also, Virginia Tech's Mary C. Holliman brought keen editorial judgement to these pages, to my benefit. With pleasure and thanks I acknowledge also Dr. Raymond D. Smoot, Jr. and Mode A. Johnson of the Virginia Tech Foundation. It was their idea, based on a book about Washington's Willard Hotel, to produce an informal history of Hotel Roanoke; it was they who invited me to write it, and it was they who gave me encouragement and support every word of the way. With me were Dianne Smith, the book's talented designer, and Bruce Muncy who contributed original photography for the book and other work on the project. To those I have listed and to those I may have overlooked, go my thanks for bringing life and flavor to the rambling heap of stone, brick and wood known as Hotel Roanoke.

Feci quod potui, meliora potentes.

Donlan Piedmont
Roanoke
Winter, 1993-Summer, 1994

The Palm Court, later Oval Room, in 1947

PREFACE

By

Marshall Fishwick, Ph.D

Professor of Humanities and Communications Studies
Virginia Tech

"Would you like to have dinner at the Hotel?"

For a young Roanoker growing up during the Great Depression, that meant more than dinner at the Hotel Roanoke. It meant nearly heaven.

In a time of austerity, it meant opulence. In a time of scarcity, it meant abundance. In a time of drabness, it meant beauty. Hotel Roanoke, on a high hill, smacked of another world. Dinner at the Hotel? Who wouldn't want to go to Camelot?

Looking down on the emerging sooty city, and the rail lines which were its life blood, the hotel was formal while our lives were functional. We built with pine, but the Hotel used polished English walnut and carved oak. We had naked light bulbs—the Hotel had chandeliers. And wonder of wonders— could you believe it— a light went on automatically when you opened the closets!

I was born not far from the Hotel, though I didn't go there often. Still it loomed large in my mind, as do castles and cathedrals for Europeans. Roanoke was the Magic City, and this was the spot where magic was turned into reality.

The Hotel was born with the city in 1882, when a lonely spot once inhabited largely by deer seeking salt at Big Lick set out to be a railroad boom town. The railroad came, and so did the Viscose plant which we proudly called "the largest silk mill in the world." The British-owned Viscose hired many officials (including my father) from England. Was it not right, then, that Hotel Roanoke should be built in the Tudor style? Didn't King Charles II call Virginia his Old Dominion?

The service, the accommodations, and the food were exceptional. The landmark dishes gave Donlan Piedmont the title of this book— peanut soup and spoonbread— and he preserves both recipes in Appendix B. Try them.

But what can never be reproduced in today's styrofoam and plastic world is the ambiance, the sense of splendor, almost of wonder that we once felt when we entered. There was the great chandelier, bedecked with its pineapple, symbol of hospitality; the lobby paneled in black walnut; the black marble tables; the Chinese sideboard; and portraits of our two Virginia demigods, General Washington and General Lee. There was the Writing Room, the Oval Room, and the Crystal Ballroom, green, red, and gold. This was somehow not only beautiful but sacred space.

And the murals! So far as I know, they were our only public ones. They were sentimental, unhistorical, and wonderful: John Smith marrying Pocahontas, Patrick Henry captivating the Assembly, the plantation thriving. Here was mythic Virginia, where the birds warbled sweet in the springtime.

God was in that heaven, and all was right with the world.

No wonder the rich and famous came here: John D. Rockefeller, J.P. Morgan (who liked the scrambled eggs), Jack Dempsey, Jeanette MacDonald, Dwight Eisenhower, Richard Nixon, George Bush, and many more. This book demonstrates how a building can be one of the keys to the social and cultural life of our country.

One social event that I shall always remember was the "Gone With the Wind" ball, held at the Hotel when that movie came out in 1939, a bonanza for the local American Theater. I was too young to go and hear the music (was it by the Roanoke Machine Shops Orchestra?), but I recall pictures of the local dandies, peacock-proud, dressed like Rhett Butlers, their gold chains dangling as they walked. No wonder the local Scarlet O'Haras waited with bated breath as their fans fluttered.

Far away in Europe the world waited as Hitler invaded Poland and set off World War II, unlike any Washington or Lee could have imagined. Like many young Virginians, I left for that War from the N & W station, just across from the Hotel Roanoke. It was a cold night, and I was joining the navy. My father gave me a pair of long red woolen underwear, bought at nearby Oak Hall's. He had been to sea, and he knew I would need them. I did. As my train pulled out of the station, I looked at the Hotel on the hill. I carried that flickering view with me throughout the war.

In the post-war years the Hotel grew old, like those of us who had admired it for decades; and as Donlan Piedmont tells us, it seemed doomed for death. Not so. This is a tale of revival and renewal. The Hotel Roanoke story is a story worth telling and it is told well. Find out now for yourself.

The Lobby in the 1950s

Snow scene, 1958

HOTEL MORIBUNDIS

One day towards the end of November 1989, a man, whose name, alas, is not known, came up to the front door of Hotel Roanoke, plugged his electric drill into a long extension cord, and began efficiently to make history. In minutes—20 possibly, 30 at the most—he had installed a sturdy lock on the right-hand door, just above the shiny brass plate. For the first time in its 107-year history, the stately, cherished old Hotel Roanoke had taken steps to keep people out.

Thus the whine and whirr of an electrical device supplied a shrill lamentation to accompany the Hotel's last days. The unthinkable had occurred, and the old place, carrying its gentle burden of tradition and fame and glories would in a few days go out of business. It would not—indeed, could not—disappear from the tribal memory of the city that for more than a century lay under its gaze.

Hotel Roanoke – Roanoke Va
1886

Early pictures of the Hotel, late 1880s; clockwise from top: bleak, bleaker, bleakest

CHAPTER I

How They Brought The Good News From Lexington To Big Lick

Halfway between Appomattox and the 20th Century, Big Lick, Virginia, in 1881 was an unremarkable place. The 1880 census listed 669 persons and about 100 houses, fairly evenly divided between black and white residents. It had but one important business street, and that one unpaved and punctuated with stepping stones as crossings. Chartered as a town in 1874, Big Lick had a newspaper—the *Roanoke Leader*—and a railroad—the Atlantic, Mississippi & Ohio, the ambitiously named and at the time virtually bankrupt creature of General William Mahone. The town's principal industry seems to have been based on tobacco, for there were six factories, one producing cigars. This place with the unsophisticated name lay between Hollins College to the north and Roanoke College to the west, even then long-established and highly regarded institutions.

Great events involving the railroad were in the process of fruition and the visionaries of Big Lick were quick to see the possibilities. Frederick J. Kimball, president of the Shenandoah Valley Railroad, and himself a world-class visionary, was looking for an appropriate spot where his north-south SVRR could cross the east-west line of the AM&O. The AM&O was bought for $8,505,000 by the same Philadelphia interests which owned the SVRR and the owners quickly combined the two into the Norfolk and Western Railroad. In time, Kimball would serve as the NW's president on two separate occasions. and was responsible for opening up the Pocahontas coalfields to Norfolk and Western traffic. That was yet to come, however.

The proposed intersection of the two railroads was hardly confidential, for surveyors were already busy looking at various routes in the Roanoke Valley. Aware of this, and sensing major possibilities for their town, the Big Lick establishment assembled what was surely one of the first industrial development packages of incentives, offering land and cash (either $5,000 or $10,000—there are two versions from which to choose) to the railroad to locate in Big Lick. It was delivered April 21, 1881 via overnight horseback rides by C. W. Thomas from Big Lick to Buchanan and John C. Moomaw from Buchanan to Lexington, where the Shenandoah Valley Railroad Board was meeting. The package and its rather golden evidence of Big Lick's interest had, according to Mayor Henry Trout (quoted in E. F. Striplin's *The Norfolk and Western: A History*), "a very good effect...Mr. Kimball remarked that the people of Big Lick were alive and at Big Lick the Shenandoah would have good friends."

His mind thus made up, Kimball—whom Roanokers subsequently and with good reason hailed as the man "to whom we owe so much"—saw immediately that Big Lick could not possibly absorb the enormous enterprise he was about to put in place there. Big Lick's eagerness was not enough. What was needed to complement a new and major railroad,

Above, the lobby and lobby sitters in 1932; upper right, the staircase from the lobby, photographed perhaps in the 1920s; right, The "English Beer Garden" in 1934

a general office, a large machine shop complex was a new and major city.

He took the first step in that direction after turning down an offer to re-name the town after him. "Call it Roanoke," he is supposed to have said. And he put the town's new name to an immediate and promising use by creating the Roanoke Land and Improvement Company early in 1881. Its goal was to build the city he foresaw would be essential to shelter and sustain the thousands who would flock to Roanoke to share the new prosperity which the railroad would bring. From the old Atlantic, Mississippi & Ohio would come 170; from the old Shenandoah Valley Railroad, another 200. Train service people from Lynchburg would add an additional 700, and the shops would add 100 more at first, with many hundreds more to follow. It was a lot of people to absorb, but Roanoke Land and Improvement Company was nothing if not optimistic— and prepared.

By 1881 the company held options on several hundred acres, acquired rather cheaply before the decision to set up headquarters was announced, and planned to acquire more. And not only to acquire the land, but to lay out on it streets for residences, commercial establishments and the machine shops where the railroad could repair and even build its own cars and locomotives (particular classes of which were described a century later as the "finest steam locomotives ever built"). Soon the company organized water and gas utilities.

Roanoke Land and Improvement Company published advertisements in the *Roanoke Leader* for the sale of building lots "for all purposes." Looking ahead, the company declared that "The rapid development of the town renders this a particularly desirable point for store-keepers and mechanics to locate" and predicted that the railroad's shops "will give employment to 1000 mechanics," an ambitious but not impossible figure, as things turned out. For buyers of the lots, there were "very reasonable terms."

And so there were. Lots 25 by 90 feet cost $350; 70 by 130 feet, $600 (although some were tagged at $750). Lots on "hilly land" could be bought for as little as $100. The railroad sold lots to builders and contracted with builders for houses on its own lots for railroad officials. In November 1881, in a letter to Kimball, H. L Moore, an active builder in those heady days, reported the need for "the several streets of Roanoke 926 shade trees, placing ten trees to every block of 400 feet on each side of the street." Striplin writes that "between February 1881 and June 1882, the N&W or its subsidiaries erected 78 frame and 60 brick houses, and individuals, on lots bought from the company, erected a mill, two office buildings, 15 stores and seven dwelling houses."

P. L. Terry, one of the town's leaders and a subscriber to the fund that played a part in luring the railroad, advertised in the *Leader* that he had for sale "on the Installment Plan or for Cash, twelve newly built, nicely finished and well arranged houses with eight and ten rooms in each." Installment payments would be "$40 per month and no interest," an arrangement difficult to resist. He also advertised "Fifty Choice Building Lots" in a neighborhood through which Jefferson Street ran and "where several of our best citizens have already located."

In the same period, Striplin notes, the number of Roanoke

"The rapid development of the town renders this a particularly desirable point for store-keepers and mechanics to locate..."

blacksmiths increased from three to seven, doctors from four to ten, lawyers from two to six and saloons from two to twelve. One new church brought the city's total to six and the number of dwellings for the faithful and heathen alike increased from 58 to 268. In spite of the secular growth, "the single jail still sufficed." He observed also that the number of hotels had grown from three to nine.

One of those nine was Hotel Roanoke. Its forthcoming construction was signalled in the land company's original prospectus of February 1881: "...and also to build and equip a hotel—capacity about 20 rooms." Thus Hotel Roanoke was not a corporate afterthought decided upon to ride the crest of a boomtown wave, but an integral element in the town's development plan. Kimball himself selected the site in a wheat field on a hill north of the city and above the railroad tracks. City fathers, though pleased at the prospect of a new and almost-certain-to-be-grand hotel, would have preferred it to be elsewhere. Clare White, in her invaluable book, *Roanoke 1740-1982*, quotes Mayor Henry Trout, who had been with Kimball on that fateful occasion: "I afterward reported to our people...what I had heard. They immediately appointed me a committee of one to go and see Mr. Kimball and ask him not to put the hotel and depot there, as we were afraid it would draw the trade off Franklin Road." The measure of his persuasive skills has been on view for well over a century.

The site settled upon, work moved apace. George T. Pearson, 427 Walnut Street, Philadelphia, was the architect, his name printed with elaborate swashes on the list of construction specifications he had prepared. The design called for a Queen Anne building 177 feet long by 73 feet wide, and this had not been completed before an "annex" 132 feet long by 43 feet wide was attached. Its cost, $12,000, brought the bill for the entire project to about $60,000. There were to be 34 guest rooms in the original building instead of the 20 alluded to in the prospectus, plus 35 more in the annex.

Pearson's specifications are worth examining. He insisted, in adjective-rich imperatives, that all work was to be performed in a "true, perfect and thoroughly workmanlike manner" and with "good, proper and sufficient materials." Floor joists were to be 3 by 12 inches, cellar girders 12 by 12, all sturdy timber and all yellow pine. The porch ceilings were to have two coats of linseed oil and "cleaned of all pencil marks and other defects; all hard wood work to be finished with Berry's Hand Oil Finish."

Brass bolts were to be installed on all inside doors and iron on all entrance doors. Speaking tubes were to run from the office to the kitchen and to servants' rooms. Kitchen specifications called for a seven-foot "French oven," two fires, two ovens and a 36-inch wrought iron furnace. An 18-inch portable furnace, made of "Russia iron," was installed in the bar.

Partitions in the privies were to be made of "beaded boards and the rooms lined with same; doors to be slat panel with spring hinges; seats to be 1-1/2 inches thick." These facilities were to be served by the first sewer line built in Roanoke, which ran from the Hotel and emptied into Lick Run, east of the building.

In May 1882, with construction already in progress, Roanoke Land and Improvement awarded a contract for one million bricks to G. H. Adams and Bros. of Lynchburg.

South wing, circa 1920s

Left, the Hotel in 1910, displaying a huge flag; lower left, a typical guest room of the late teens or early 1920s; below, the Dining Room, 1937

Upper left, the aptly named Sun Room, 1910; upper right, the elevator bank and murals, 1938; lower left, the airy Green Room of 1932, and lower right, the Colonial Room, formerly the Palm Court, later the Oval Room, in 1947

The bricks—9-1/2 inches long, 4 1/2 inches wide and 2-7/8 inches thick—were to be manufactured in Roanoke, part by hand, part by machine. They were to be delivered to the site at the rate of 40,000 each week, and the contract price was $8.50 per thousand. A million bricks are a great many bricks indeed, far more, one would think, than the number required for what was essentially a wooden structure. Possibly Roanoke Land and Improvement, taking advantage of what was later called "economics of scale," bought them for later use in the construction of brick residences mentioned earlier.

There exists in the pages of the *Roanoke Leader* a thorough if breathless description of Hotel Roanoke as it stood in October 1882. It had begun receiving guests that same month, although the official opening was not to take place until Christmas Day. The writer was escorted on the tour by "H. Chapman, Esq, the polite and attentive superintendent of the Roanoke Land and Improvement Company."

In the basement was a barbershop "with bathrooms attached, all fully equipped and supplied with hot and cold water and finished up in handsome style." Next to the barbershop was a furnace room with a hot air furnace "of large capacity" supported by three coal rooms, each 30 by 40 feet. Sharing the basement space were "large, finely finished bar rooms, in which we observed large fireplaces of pressed brick after the Queen Anne style, which is the architectural style of the entire building." The basement also housed essential hotel functions, a steam laundry and the bakery, with an eight-foot by six-foot oven.

The dining room—"saloon" in the vocabulary of the 1880s—was "extremely handsome" and could seat 200 under six

chandeliers of eight lights each. Like the office and public parts of the building, the dining room was finished in hand rubbed and polished English walnut, carved oak, cherry and ash. The dining room was served by a butler's pantry (with "electric and speaking tube connections") and a kitchen "completely equipped with all appliances and aids to the culinary art." The range consisted of two fire boxes, three large ovens, and an "immense broiler and boiler of great size." A dozen floor-to-ceiling closets housed the china and were "fitted up with apparatus for warming dishes."

The new Hotel sought to offer elegance along with up-to-date conveniences. All guest rooms featured hot and cold running water, and many had zinc or porcelain bathtubs, said to be among the first in Roanoke, at least where one could bathe in a "warm and private place." An interconnected and complicated system of bells and speaking tubes permitted guests to direct their various wishes to the staff. By means of a small ebony knob in the room, the guest could call a bellboy (one ring), chambermaid (two rings), ice water (three rings) or hot water (four rings). An elevator ran to the third floor from the basement, and for those who chose not to put their trust in the system of ropes and pulleys that supplied its motive power, there was "a grand stair ornamented with carved and polished oak and lighted by a handsome stained glass window."

The attentive Mr. Chapman told the writer that five hundred trees had been ordered for the grounds, which were being graded at the time and would be lighted by nearly two dozen gas lamps. The mention of such a large number of trees might have been puffery on the part of the Roanoke Land and Improvement superintendent, for there is no evidence that such a forest ever graced the ten-acre site.

"...we observed large fireplaces of pressed brick after the Queen Anne style, which is the architectural style of the entire building."

Three views accenting certain forgotten features of the Hotel of the past: an odd little tower facing the west, date unknown; cheerful striped awnings, facing south, 1920, and the verandas, shaded with vines, probably photographed in the teens

"Taken in its entirety," the Hotel was, the *Leader* concluded, "one of the most commodious, well arranged, and handsomely finished hotels we have ever seen outside of a few of our largest cities. There is one feature, however, in which it cannot be excelled, and that is the

MAGNIFICENT VIEW

presented from the verandas and every window and door in the building. The view needs to be seen to be appreciated. We have neither the ability or space to depict it in words. On every hand the horizon is met by mountains of attractive outline, while the landscape intervening is beautiful and attractive...This cannot fail to become a most popular resort, and under the experienced management of the lessee, Mr. Mullin, will soon become famous with the traveling public and visitors to our growing city."

This Mr. Mullin is a shadowy figure. His name does not appear in the accustomed references about the Hotel. In its 50th Anniversary Edition (November 30, 1936), the *Roanoke Times* says the first manager was George L. Jacoby, succeeded in 1888 by Fred Foster. Foster was also the manager of smaller hotels the railroad owned in Bluefield, West Virginia and Pulaski, Virginia. Between 1893 and 1901, the manager was S. K. Campbell, replaced in the latter year by Foster again; and when Foster died, his widow assumed the managership. Subsequent managers will be cataloged in appropriate places as this narrative proceeds.

An 1882 photograph of the completed Hotel Roanoke shows it stark and rather bleak, landscaped with a few bushes here and there, and no sign of the 500 trees Mr. Chapman had promised. The Hotel's half-timber, half-stucco appearance it retained all its life was clearly established. The "annex" formed one leg of a right angle, parallel to the railroad tracks. Its roof, pierced by dormers, sloped gently down to protect covered verandas, already partially concealed by vines, running the length of the building on both floors. The other leg of the building faced Jefferson Street, and seemed to be all gables, projections, more porches and even the suggestion of a gambrel roof. Guests entered the grounds through a gate at the corner of Jefferson Street and Shenandoah Avenue driveway and followed a sweeping path to the entrance, located approximately at the point where the two legs of the angle met.

It was through that entrance that Roanokers flocked in 1882 to celebrate with Christmas dinner the formal opening of the Hotel. For a new hotel in a community whose

This gate led to the Hotel from the corner of Shenandoah Avenue and Jefferson Street, or somewhere close to it.

rough edges had not yet been smoothed down, it was a haute monde event. There were nine courses on the menu:,

MERRY CHRISTMAS

SOUPS
Chicken a la reine   Consomme
*

BOILED
Turkey, celery sauce   Mutton, a la sauce
*

COLD DISHES
Boned Turkey en aspic   Ham
Chicken Salad   Lobster Salad
*

ENTREES
Filet de Boeuf pique aux champigons
Petit Pate of Oyster   Lobster
Diamondback Terrapin a la St. Cloud
Timbal of Macaroni a la Nelson
*

ROAST
Rib of Beef   Turkey and Cranberry Sauce
Young Pig   Goose and Applesauce
*

VEGETABLES
Mashed Potatoes   Green Peas   Sweet Potatoes
Tomatoes   Corn
*

PASTRY
English Plum Pudding, Brandy Sauce
Apple Pie   Mince Pie   Peach Pie
Lemon Meringue Pie
*

DESSERT
Pound Cake   Fruit Cake   English Wafers
French Kisses   Lady Fingers
Vanilla Ice Cream   Wine Jelly
*

FRUITS
Figs   Oranges
Bananas   Malaga Grapes   Raisins
Pecans   Almonds   English Walnuts
*

Coffee   Chocolate   Tea
Cheese

The price attached to this sumptuous bill of fare is unknown, but it surely included the costs of bringing the more exotic foods into Roanoke by train from more sophisticated centers like Washington, Richmond, or possibly even New York. More important than the cost was the clear identification of the new Hotel as the center of elegance and hospitality in the new city and the source of pleasure and profit for the Hotel.

Few could have known it, but with that dinner, the Hotel Roanoke mystique and tradition began, and the second knot in the silken rope that eventually bound the Hotel and the city together was tied just a year or so after the official opening.

Roanoke's young bloods, newcomers to the town with the railroad and its associated activities and restless for a social life, had begun to look to the Hotel Roanoke as its locus and beyond the city limits for much of their companionship. They organized the German Club, arranged for its first dance and invited dates from more or less nearby cities and counties. Accompanied by their chaperones, the young women came—by rail, on reduced-fare tickets—and "were installed at the Hotel Roanoke...at the expense of the local swains."

This opening "German" was subsequently described in the columns of the *Leader* as "the most brilliant and recherche society event that has yet occurred in our city." Since Roanoke was only just emerging from its wooden sidewalk stage, this claim in truth could hardly have meant much.

The festivities began at 9 to the "sweet strains" of the Roanoke Machine Shops Orchestra. By then, "the parlors were thronged with the beauty and fashion of our city, supplemented by charming representatives from different portions of the state as well as abroad. All were in full evening costume, the sombre dress suits of the men contrasting prettily with the warm colors of the ladies' costumes...The ballroom was handsomely decorated, brilliantly illuminated and seemed to mirror the happiness and pleasure so clearly expressed in the face of each participant in the many and intricate figures."

No doubt, but such happiness and pleasure were of necessity confined to the dance floor and the parlors, and not mirrored elsewhere. For Number 12 in the Club's by-laws for 1883 stated unambiguously that "Members shall not be allowed to go upon the second floor of the Hotel during the evening of a German, but must leave their partners at the first landing of the stairs, where they will be met by a maid especially appointed for that purpose." Some years, the revels continued the next day with a "morning German" that ended only when the imports and their chaperones took the train home.

In the 1938 remodeling, the ceiling of the Oval Room required 18 coats of dark blue paint

In the 1880s and '90s, the Germans were formal affairs, featuring mostly the "graceful, stately waltz", although there was a generous sprinkling of polkas and gavottes as well. In the decades that followed, the dance program, abandoning the gavottes, reflected the fads and tastes of the day: the frug, bunny hug, jitterbug, turkey trot, foxtrot, Charleston, conga, samba, rumba, and others, some now as forgotten as the sarabande and as passé as the minuet.

In the earlier days, decorations were "simple in the handsome ballroom of the Hotel Roanoke, but the dances were gay and brilliant functions." Orchestras might come from Richmond, favors from New York, refreshments from Philadelphia. In later years, there were five Germans each season: Opening. Thanksgiving, New Year's, Mid-winters and Easters.

"German" Dance Card

> *"...mama and papa used to dress in costume to attend the German Club Masquerade Balls at the Hotel."*

Very likely many of the same musicians who made up the Roanoke Machine Works Orchestra also played in its band, which in the early days of the 20th century gave afternoon concerts on the Hotel lawn. The appearance of the grounds had been steadily improving from the bare, stark look following the building's completion. The effect was due to the energy of a man named Patrick Foy. A friend of Kimball, he supervised the building of a stone wall around the property (where parts of it remain in place to this day),

Helen and Broaddus Chewning, parents of Helen Chewning Fitzpatrick, costumed for one of the traditional "Germans"

undertook major plantings of trees and flower beds, and built at the Hotel the first greenhouse in the city. Foy cared strongly about that greenhouse. On September 16, 1890, he wrote a pencilled note to a Mr. Churchill of the Norfolk and Western Railroad's Engineering Department. "From all appearances, we are going to have an early fall," he wrote, adding diffidently, "I think it would be well to make some Provisions for the Heating of the Green House as soon as possible." Then with a touch of asperity, he finished: "There is also some 6 glass (window panes) Broken which ought to be repaired at once and the doors can hardly be Shut from the way they are Swelled." It was signed "Yours Truly, Pat Foy."

Generous with the railroad's funds when it came to the greenhouse, he was careful, even frugal, when it came to himself. His expense account for the month of August 1890 (submitted on buff stationery with "Hotel Roanoke, Roanoke, Virginia, Fred E. Foster, Manager," printed ornately in blue) totaled $9.00. It covered four days in Bluefield, two in Lynchburg and one in Pulaski.

He died at the age of 80 in 1924, one of the last links of the Hotel to its origins. (But not the last. That distinction belongs to J. Ed Brown, headwaiter, who joined the Hotel staff in 1882, and 62 years later was still on the job,

Undated photograph, perhaps from the turn of the century, showing the rail crossing at Jefferson Street

"...broad porches, clad with Virginia Creeper, form one of the most restful and agreeable spots in the entire city."

and making a good thing out of autographing the Regency Room menu featuring his photograph.)

Through all of this, the tradition of the German continued. From time to time, there was a variation from the traditional black- (or even white-) tie events. Helen Fitzpatrick of Roanoke remembers "when mama and papa used to dress in costume to attend the German Club Masquerade Balls at the Hotel." Austin Neal, who was the Club president in 1934, remembers going to one of the Masquerades as a Spaniard—"a blond Spaniard"—with trousers tucked into high boots and a white shirt with big sleeves.

At the Germans during Prohibition years, he recalls, the band would be playing away cheerfully, but the dance floor was empty. "They were all off somewhere drinking." This was a significant departure from the Victorian rectitude that had installed By-law No. 12, which in any case had by that time been repealed. Once, a heavy snow made it impossible for Neal and his wife Betty to leave after the dance, so they spent the night at the Hotel, and returned home the next morning still wearing their evening clothes, "an interesting sight for the neighbors."

(Another of Neal's memorable experiences with the Hotel involves a high school banquet in 1926. "At the end," he recalled, "there was this little coffee spoon by my plate. So I put it in my pocket as a sort of souvenir. The next morning, my father saw it on my dresser, and there was an uncomfortable conversation with him. He told me I had to take it back, that it wasn't mine to have. Since he worked in the railroad offices across the street, I asked him if he wouldn't take it back for me. 'No. You took it. You return it,' he said. So I went in to the lobby, thinking that everyone there

recognized me as the well-known spoon thief. I laid that spoon on the registration desk and ran out.")

The first duty of the German's new president was to make arrangements for the next season's dances. "I called on Ken Hyde or George Denison to fix the dates and with Charles Hofer to arrange the menus," Neal said later, invoking three of the great names in the Hotel's pantheon. "Being president was not an arduous chore."

Long before Neal's adventures in the Hotel, patronage was steadily growing and for good reason. The Hotel was becoming established as more than a place to spend a night, especially to families. It sought to carve a niche in the resort market, which in the latter part of the century was a growing one. Well-to-do-families left the summer heat of the cities in search of fresh mountain air, relaxation and all the spiritual refreshment which flows from the proximity of pristine nature. Hotel Roanoke had just that combination, as a promotional brochure from 1885—just three years after the Hotel opened—made clear, plus its own elegance. It had become "...a most delightful resort, not only during the summer months, but throughout the year. It has a cuisine acceptable to the most fastidious and affords every comfort to be found at home. (It is) within reach of the Natural Bridge, Peaks of Otter and other attractive places, to which delightful excursions can be made." Guests ever since have made the same "delightful excursions."

Not too much later, the Roanoke Chamber of Commerce had this to say in a promotional piece of its own:

>...although for the past year her capabilities for entertainment have been often put to the test,

Greyhound bus at the Hotel's entrance. Railroad's General Office Building and automobiles date this photograph to the early or mid 30s

the city is well provided. The pioneer of the large hotels is Hotel Roanoke, owned by the Norfolk and Western Railroad Company and located opposite the depot upon an elevation which makes it a prominent object from any approach. The architecture is of a cottage-like character, with an abundance of piazza space. It is not too much to say that broad porches, clad with

Virginia Creeper, form one of the most restful and agreeable spots in the entire city. There are few hotels north or south affording a more beautiful outlook. At the present time a large and costly addition is being built on the western side, and when this is done, the 'Roanoke' will contain 150 bedrooms and will have a frontage to the south of 300 feet. It is under the management of

Mr. Fred E. Foster, who also has charge of the Norfolk and Western Railway's 'Inns' at Radford, Pulaski and Bluefield.

An unidentified patron about this time wrote about the Hotel in terms which have since been widely quoted. It was "a splendid hotel crowning the hill in the midst of lawns, parterres of flowers and ceaseless fountains...The parlor is as pretty a room as you will find in many a mile, and the dining room light and cheerful...The table and service are of a high order...and I do not know a better resting place...between Philadelphia and Florida."

Norfolk and Western trains entered the city bringing passengers from all points, foreign and domestic, attracted to the Hotel by such persuasive and seductive rhetoric. The Shenandoah Valley line had connections through Hagerstown to cities of the Northeast, including especially New York. The main line ran from Norfolk, with steamer connections to European and Atlantic ports. Guests from the south came by rail from connections at Winston-Salem, Durham and Bristol, and from Washington via Lynchburg. Porters met these trains and escorted passenger-guests out of the station, across the street and up a shady path that led to the Hotel's inviting porches and canopied entrance.

The reference in the Chamber of Commerce brochure to the city's hotels being "put to the test" referred principally to an expansion of the Hotel Roanoke in 1891, which added a number of bedrooms and remodeled extensively the part of the hotel that faced west. The timber-stucco motif was continued and a large wraparound porch built to face both west and south. The work, from an accounting point of view, increased the book value of the property

from $45,000 to $125,000, certainly a significant investment for the time.

Hotel Roanoke faced a much sterner test in 1898, when, around 1:30 on the afternoon of July 1, a fire broke out in the kitchen and quickly spread through the frame structure. A photograph taken from across the railroad tracks shows smoke pouring from a half-dozen orifices, and the lawn filled with spectators and littered with materials salvaged—or at least thrown—from the burning building. The *Roanoke Times*, recalled the event in its 50th anniversary edition of November 30, 1936.

> As the blaze soared and it was evident that the fire department was unable to control it, hundreds of men rushed in from the Roanoke Machine Works and assisted in saving much of the furniture and carpets and destroying thousands of dollars worth of hotel equipment in their efforts to save something from the flames. Beds, dressers, mattresses and other furniture, including bowls and pitchers with which many of the rooms were equipped, were hurled from the second and third floor windows, while carpets were wrenched from the floors and piled out in the greatest confusion. Willing hands on the outside were ready to drag the furnishings to vantage points on the lawn to the south and west of the blazing building, all of which was practically destroyed with the exception of the east wing. The roof of the west wing was burned and the interior was gutted. The lobby and office were disfigured by flames, but the construction held intact.

The 1898 fire attracted hundreds of sightseers and shut the Hotel down for several months

22nd Annual Convention of Va. Association of Local Fire Ins. Agts. Roanoke, Va Sept. 22-23, 1920

The Virginia Association of Local Fire Insurance Agents met in the Hotel in 1920

There is no record of injuries, even in the face of the putative helpers' misplaced zeal.

For a time it was feared that the entire hotel would have to be rebuilt, but this turned out to be a too-pessimistic view. It was shut down for several months while repair work continued, and by the end of September, a limited number of guests began returning. In October, a double wedding was held to signal, in effect, that the Hotel was again open for business.

For a few weeks, such guests as were registered took their meals in the railroad depot dining room. Although not affiliated in any way with the Hotel, its cuisine was of a quality to give the place a reputation for good dining. Carter Burgess, a prominent Roanoker, was an aide to General Dwight D. Eisenhower in the Second World War, and subsequently a notable figure in American industry— and incidentally, son-in-law of the late R. H. Smith, former president of the Norfolk and Western Railway. He has remembered being taken to dinner there by his father, an employee of the Railway Express Company. It was, he said, his father's "idea of a treat" during the Depression. He recalled that during this time Railway Express was one of the offices which moved into the Hotel because of an inability to pay their own rent in those difficult days.

Although the railroad was forced to shut the Hotel down temporarily and take the loss of revenue, there was never a thought of closing it. After only 16 years, Hotel Roanoke was already firmly situated as a Roanoke institution with a ripening if not exactly mature tradition and the railroad owners were determined to hold the course.

So the hotel that sprang from the blackened ruins was

rebuilt...and rebuilt...and rebuilt in one form or another over the next 60 years or so. What with new wings, alterations and additions, there was left at the end only a globe chandelier said to have been in the original building for posterity to touch or even see. In 1916, the old East Wing was torn down and replaced with a new three-story, 72-room addition. Most of the bedrooms were equipped with private baths and a number of private dining rooms were installed as well.

By 1931, even this relatively new addition was out of date with the increasing spate of automobile travel. The railroad was willing to spend substantially—$225,000—in this Depression year to make its showpiece more attractive. (Norfolk and Western was in a bullish mood, for simultaneously it was putting up a new eight-story office building across the street from the Hotel, immediately north of the 1896 offices.) For that money, it added to the Hotel 40,000 square feet of floor space, 75 rooms (for a total of 250 in the entire Hotel) and a 60-car garage. The garage was not the only gesture to advancing technology. Rooms were equipped with electric fans, movable telephones which could be plugged in at four different locations; large closets which lighted automatically when the door was opened, a combination shower and tub bath, and running ice water. All this, reported the *Norfolk and Western Magazine*, put Hotel Roanoke "in a position to enter its 50th year and all the years to come with adequate accommodations and increased comforts for a patronage which has grown steadily since its rambling old ancestor looked down upon the vigorous beginnings of a new city in 1882."

Increased comfort, certainly, for that was the always-moving goal of the Hotel; but "adequate accommodations" widely

H. W. Shields, vice president and general manager of Pocahontas Coal & Coke Company, and his daughter, Mrs. Anna Hewitt, mother of 15-year-old Henry. The Shields family were the first occupants of the penthouse apartment created in the 1938 remodeling

Rooms 128 and 129 – reserved for Hollins College women

Steelwork for the 1937-38 work takes shape

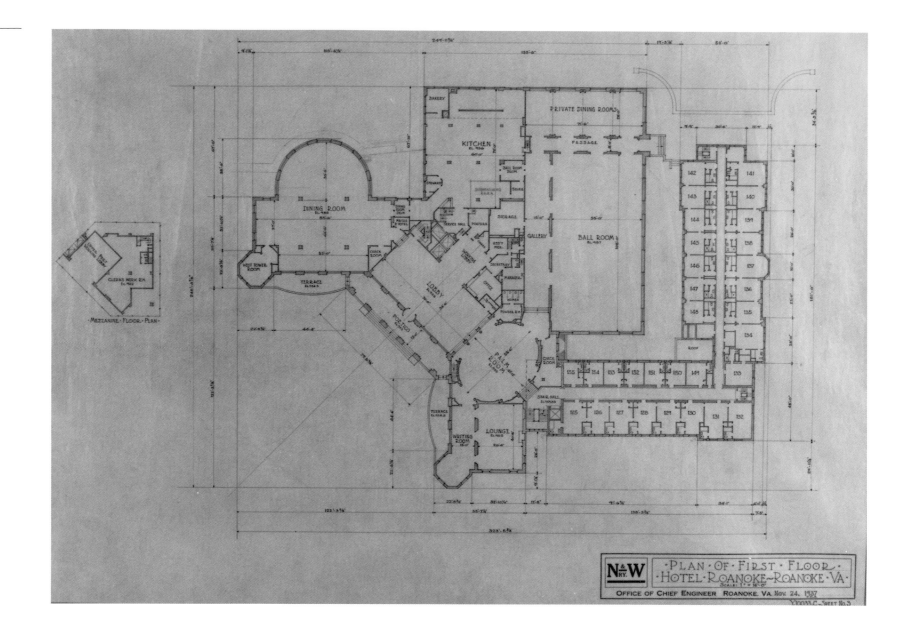

MEZZANINE FLOOR PLAN

CLERKS WORK RM.
EL. 122

DINING ROOM
EL. 105.0

WEST TOWER
ROOM

TERRACE
EL. 104.5

KITCHEN
EL. 106

BAKERY

PRIVATE DINING ROOMS

PASSAGE

BALL ROOM
ROOM

DISHWASHING ROOM

STORAGE

GALLERY

BALL ROOM
EL. 105

SERVICE HALL

PORTERS

CHECK ROOM

WOMEN'S TOILETS

ASST. MGR.

SECRETARY

MANAGER

OFFICE

WOMEN

POWDER RM.

LOBBY

PORTICO

PALM ROOM

CHECK ROOM

CHECK ROOM

GALLERY

TERRACE
EL. 104.5

STAIR HALL

WRITING ROOM

LOUNGE
EL. 105

142   141

143   140

144   139

145   138

146   137

147   136

148   135

134

155 154 153 152 151 150 149   133

ROOF

125 126 127 128 129 130 131 132

N&W
RY.

PLAN OF FIRST FLOOR
HOTEL ROANOKE ~ ROANOKE VA
SCALE 1" = 16'-0"
OFFICE OF CHIEF ENGINEER ROANOKE, VA. NOV. 24, 1937
X0033.C — SHEET No. 5

missed the mark. Only seven years later came the major rebuilding program, budgeted at $1,050,000, exclusive of furnishings. The $225,000 spent for the 1931 work, on the other hand, including furnishings. What came out of the 1937-38 work was symbolized by the grand Tudor entrance, at once imposing and embracing. It was this image of Hotel Roanoke which was photographed, sketched or carried away in the memories of all who passed through the doors.

Still, what was taken away had a memorable charm of its own. The old deep porches, shaded by vines, were charming gathering spots for guests—and others. Elizabeth Bowles, later a Roanoke City Councilwoman and one of the principal missionaries in the successful effort to bring the Miss Virginia Pageant to the Hotel, said that in her teens she would persuade her father to take her the Hotel so she could sit in a porch rocker. Bill Gearhart on Saturday afternoons would climb over the railings and chat with a railroad official who lived in the Hotel. "He was always good for a quarter, so I could go to the movies," Gearhart told an interviewer. Fred Walker, who came to the Hotel as director of sales in 1962, had "heard stories of how certain representatives of the world's oldest profession would come over to the Hotel and sit on the porch, sip lemonade and, for all I know, complete various business arrangements." Years later, Walker was visited in his office by a woman, who, though attractive, was to a critical eye perhaps a trifle past the blush of youth. She said that she and two of her ladies were on their way to Florida, and she wondered if perhaps the Hotel would be interested in...well, you know. Courteously and firmly, Walker declined to discuss any such proposal. No, he said, the Hotel was not and never was interested in...well, you know. The woman took the rebuff in good spirit, saying "well, no harm trying," and departed the premises.

George B. Post and Sons, a New York architectural firm whose speciality was hotel design, rebuilt the entire west wing. Sweeping away the old porches, the architects moved the main entrance a few degrees from south to southwest, added 181 guest rooms on five floors and a penthouse and used 524,000 bricks, a thousand tons of structural steel and 5,500 cubic yards of concrete in the process. It was also the first hotel in the country to be engineered for air-conditioning. The job included a new 100-car garage, a large number of parking spaces and tasteful landscaping. Inside, the designers created a new lobby and reception area, Dining Room, Pine Room, Writing Room, Palm Court and a ballroom.

Outside, there was to be "a veritable oasis amidst business and industry" as announced by its creator, A. A. Farnham, the Harvard-trained professor of landscape architecture at Virginia Polytechnic Institute. Its principal feature was a large—145 feet by 120 feet—formal garden behind the Dining Room, planted with 6,000 tulip bulbs and quantities of perennials and roses, with mimosa trees shading the walkways through the garden. The gardens were shielded from the sight and sound of bordering city streets by hedges and trees. It was planned as a quiet spot "for teas, meetings of garden clubs and for possible use by convention groups. In later years, a high-ranking officer of the railroad, viewing the garden from his office window across the street, would sometimes call the manager to report that unauthorized persons were in the garden picking flowers and ought to be stopped immediately. The landscaping also including the installation of a reflecting pool in front of the entrance. It was 35 feet in diameter, set in the middle of a

Around this reflecting pool in later years, Miss Virginia candidates ritually gathered for the traditional swimsuit photograph...

...people danced, cattle lowed, diners dined, politicians denounced and beauty contestants preened...

78-foot circle planted in grass, shrubs and flowers. Around this reflecting pool in later years, Miss Virginia candidates ritually gathered for their traditional swimsuit photograph, blossoms which, like the tulips in the garden, regularly caught the eye of railroad employees clustered in four or five stories of windows in the General Office Buildings.

The lobby, paneled in American black walnut an inch-and-a-half thick, was furnished for appearance and comfort. Among the conventional pieces were black marble tables 150 years old, three rosewood chairs, applewood tables, a Chinese credenza, and three chandeliers, all at least a century old. Large portraits of George Washington and Robert E. Lee, acquired in 1894, were hung on the walls.

The registration desk faced the front door. Above it was a series of murals tracing the history of the New World—the Mayflower, pilgrims and Indians, John Smith and Pocahontas marrying, Patrick Henry orating, and an old South plantation. Hung from the ceiling nearby was the 1882 globe chandelier, emblazoned with a pineapple design, the symbol of hospitality.

The Hotel's entrance before the 1938 rebuilding lay in the area around the Oval Room, then called the Palm Court, and Pine Room, and so if there was an "original" part of the building, it was here. The Palm Court was so-called because of the dozen potted palms placed on its perimeter. It was adjacent to a glassed-in porch from which guests, lounging in the wicker chairs fashionable at the time could enjoy the view of a large garden. In the 1937 remodeling, the glassed-in porch became Peacock Alley and the garden site became the Crystal Ballroom. The Palm Court, for its part, was given perhaps the most ingenious and possibly most elabo-

rate treatment in the entire remodeling. Eighteen coats of paint were applied to the ceiling to achieve the desired deep blue night sky effect, and on it was painted the configuration of celestial bodies as they appeared in the heavens November 1, 1852, the day the first train arrived in Big Lick. A green carpet, said to have been the "largest of its kind ever made," measured 54 by 41 feet. A large light hung from the middle of the ceiling over a massive, specially made table in the center of the room.

The Pine Room was paneled in warm knotty pine and hung about with traditional prints and a painting of the Roanoke Valley by a now unknown artist of the time. Two antique Windsor chairs, put together with pegs, sat for many years on either side of the black Italian marble fireplace, which like the others in the Hotel, was decorative, not functional.

The Crystal Ballroom, which would become the heart of the Hotel's business and social life, measured 46 by 118 feet, and was done in green, gold and red. Three crystal chandeliers, made in Czechoslovakia and originally fitted for gas lighting, were suspended from an arched ceiling, under which, as the years rolled by, people danced, cattle lowed, diners dined, politicians denounced and beauty contestants preened.

The Dining Room, which later earned the Mobil Four-Star award for dining excellence for eight consecutive years, like the Lobby and Oval and Pine Rooms, was located just about where it was originally, but with a new curved bay facing north and overlooking Farnham's tulip garden. It was "oyster-white in color and Georgian in design," according to a contemporary account. Dogwood, the Virginia state blossom, was used as the decorative motif and repeated in the design

The Pine Room, above, and the registration desk, circa 1947

The Fountain Room of happy memory, left; and beauty salon customers, below left, both from 1947; below right, a typical guest room in the 1931 wing

for the new china. The same account reported that the china was brought to Roanoke by rail, 1,663 dozen pieces, plus four tons of silverware.

Supporting the dining room was a new, large and state-of-the-art kitchen, including an ice machine capable of producing more than two tons of ice each day. (By coincidence, two tons was also the capacity of the new laundry.)

Upstairs, the new guest rooms—making a total of 310 in the entire Hotel— featured the new air conditioning, new furniture, indirect lighting, radio, tiled tub and shower, safety locks, "wine-colored carpets of distinctive design," and, as a final inducement, Venetian blinds plus circulating ice water. There was a penthouse, too, on the seventh floor, overlooking the city through huge gabled windows in a story-and-a-half living room. The penthouse's first tenant was H. W. Shields, vice president and general manager of Pocahontas Coal & Coke Company, who with his family lived there for many years.

That family included Roanoker Harry Hewitt, then 15, his mother, his aunt, and Shields, his grandfather. Hewitt lived in the penthouse apartment off and on for the next 25 years or so, summer vacations from boarding school and college, on leave from the Army and while working at the railroad's Roanoke Terminal. The apartment was also the first home for him and his wife Joyce for a few months in the early 1950s. (One memory from those days involves a mouse watching Joyce write thank-you notes.)

Both W. J. Jenks, the railroad's president, and E. R. Johnson, a director, and a man of substance in the community, each wanted the penthouse apartment as his own.

Shields, executive in charge of a major NW subsidiary (later the Pocahontas Land Company), pointed out that the two men's wives were both interested in gardening, and that the penthouse, for all its cachet and other advantages, had no garden. He, Shields, on the other hand, cared nothing for gardening, and thus almost by default did he get the key to 701.

The Shields family in the penthouse enjoyed the same level of service as other guests. Beds were made up and fresh towels and soap were provided daily, the rooms cleaned, waste baskets emptied, and room service was only a telephone call away. Outside telephone calls cost fifteen cents (which added up to a sizable sum, Hewitt recalls, in his dating days). And like all the other guest rooms, the penthouse apartment had a daily rental rate: the two bedrooms, two baths, dining room, the "marvelous kitchen" and living room cost $9.00 a day. There was also a terrace, but ambient dust and locomotive soot made it unusable. However, some other guests in the Hotel found a way to reach the terrace for their own intimate purposes and did so, even looking into the apartment's windows until "Mother, unhappy with these goings-on, persuaded Mr. Hyde to put a special lock on the terrace door."

The Tulip Garden, 1948

Meals were not included. Shields had his breakfast—and frequently lunch—at a downtown cafeteria, sometimes accompanied by young Harry. Dinner, on the other hand, was always in the Regency Room. Jenks had decreed that there would be no reservations, so seating was first-come, first-served. Hewitt recalls many trips from the seventh floor to the Dining Room to see if there was a line of waiting diners. "Reservations or not, we somehow always had the same table," he says.

Coming in from his day's work as a railroad yard clerk, Hewitt would "clomp across the lobby in my work clothes and boots and carrying my lunch bucket to the desk to pick up my mail." And, once in the moving-out process, Joyce, thanks to a balky elevator, found herself crossing the lobby with a dishpan full of cleaning materials for their new home, two unusual counterpoints to the Hotel's elegance.

All that was in the future when the Hotel's new look was officially unveiled to the world on September 15, 1938, just about a year from the day the Norfolk and Western announced the project. The *Roanoke Times* of the day before, from which much in this account has been taken, published a series of congratulatory advertisements from the Hotel's contractors and other well-wishers. Among them were comradely greetings from the Patrick Henry and Ponce de Leon Hotels. Kimbalton Lime Company of Shawsville praised the Hotel and its building contractor. J. A. Jones Construction Company, for "A 'Beautiful' Hotel and a 'Beautiful' Piece of Brickwork." Smithfield Packing Co., Inc., mentioned that the Hotel would be using its products in the dining room; Mick or Mack, "Roanoke-owned Grocers" declared that "It is our sincere pleasure, and unsolicited, to extend congratulatory greetings." And

so on, from the Murphy Door Bed Company through Densmore Poultry Farms to a dozen more, eager to pay for the privilege of associating themselves in public with the splendid new-

old Hotel on the Hill.

A half-page ad was from the Hotel itself, announcing open house hours (10 a.m. to 5 p.m.) for the next day, and listing prices for its meals in its "stately Main Dining Room." Breakfast ranged from 35 cents to 75 cents; luncheon from 60 cents to 90 cents, and dinner from $1.10 to $1.50. Respective menus were not shown. Rates for the rooms in the new wing began at $3.00 and in the East Wing at $2.50. It was signed by Kenneth R. Hyde, general manager, and George. L. Denison, resident manager, a pair to figure largely, even seminally, in the Hotel's subsequent history.

The opening celebrations were actually spread over two "Nights." The first, on September 15, was "Roanoke Night," when the parquetry floor of the Crystal Ballroom first felt the slide and shuffle of dancing feet. Don Bestor's Orchestra played, the same Don Bestor whose band was once part of Jack Benny's radio show. Tickets were limited to 500 couples and cost $3.00 each. As a notable, not to say extraordinary, community event, Roanoke Night ranked with the "initiatory German" of more than a half-century before, and to be equalled and possibly surpassed only by Governors' Night in 1967 and the Closing Banquet in 1989.

"Well, it was a grand party," wrote "Candida" (nom de plume of Dorothy Hancock, *Roanoke Times* reporter) in the next morning's newspaper, in an account curiously echoing the reporting of the first German in 1883:

The town will be talking for years to come about the night its Hotel Roanoke opened, and everybody who could get a reservation hauled out his tux or tails, or bought a new dress, as the case may be, and went to the ball. Went to dine, first,

Photographs of the parts of the hotel seldom seen by guests: opposite page, the employee cafeteria in the kitchen; this page, from upper left, inside the cashier's office, the laundry, a housekeeper storing a Murphy bed in a guest room, and kitchen staff at work

The garage, circa late 1940s

perhaps, in the magnificent rose and white dining room and then to dance to Don Bestor's music in the ballroom, and to wander between dances through Peacock Alley, in the blue light of the Palm Court, and down into the great lobby. It was a little hard to remember at times that we were really still in Roanoke—even the familiar faces on every side might have belonged to shipmates on some super luxury liner.

While giving our fancy sandals a rest, we had a fine time looking over all the new evening gowns parading past us. The girls looked mighty fine, there's no doubt about it. All the cerise and violet tones reported from the Paris openings were there, and the velvets, heavy satins and brocades the couturiers have gone mad about. We saw several hoopskirts, ranging from Tee Gregory's red plaid, which she seemed to have no trouble managing in dancing, to a black taffeta version of the Jezebel-inspired mode. Mary Wise Parrott's aqua velvet was a beauty, as was Tay Parrot's gold lame with a little bustle flounce to it. Mary Stone Moore (Miss) was lovely in a dress of white net with little pineapple slices of gathered net for trimming. Carol Clark's dress of flowing net in violet and purple was nothing short of an achievement.

Hair was up and hair was down—some intended as the former was nearer the latter before the evening waned. The main impression we gathered was that the off-the-neck style hasn't as yet been unreservedly adopted by our sister townswomen.

The gentlemen looked pretty handsome too. Even the one asleep out on the porch when the dance broke up looked rather distinguished in his slumbers.

It was a grand party. More we cannot say."

For John Eure, then a *Roanoke Times* reporter and later an editor, it was grand party too. He took his date home from the ball and got engaged. "The atmosphere certainly helped."

The second opening event was called "Hotel Men's Night," and attracted professional hoteliers from all over the state for dinner. The headliners were Governors James H. Price of Virginia and Homer A. Holt of West Virginia. W. J. Jenks, president of Norfolk and Western Railway, was there, and so was E. R. Johnson, a NW director and former president of Rotary International. The railroad was further represented by Vice President Sydney F. Small and almost certainly a cadre of lesser officials, unnamed in the press. Junius P. Fishburn, publisher of the *Roanoke Times* and its afternoon sister, the *World-News*, and a major figure in the city's business life, was the toastmaster. Rev. Dr. R. A. Lapsley, Jr., pastor of Roanoke's First Presbyterian Church, delivered the invocation. By any standard it was gathering of the mighty, neither for the first time nor the last in the Hotel's history.

"It was a grand party. More we cannot say."

Part of the Hotel's renowned hospitality staff in 1968; front, Alphonse (Alex) Alexander, George McReynolds, Billy Davis; back, Warren Webb, Lee Griffith and Chef Fred Brown, creator of Hotel Roanoke's famed peanut soup. Identity of the last man is unknown

Not All Brick, But People Too

With the unveiling of the new West Wing, Hotel Roanoke could be said to have entered its modern stage. The physical plant was superb, its location ideal, its reputation immaculate and growing. Overseeing and managing this glittering and promising property were two men who would lead in it into a new and golden age covering a quarter of a century: Sydney Small and Kenneth Hyde. Small, who had begun work for the railroad in 1911 as a $40-a-month clerk, had been named in 1935 as vice president-assistant to the president. His portfolio was principally public relations and legislative matters, and over the years he had managed them both so successfully that the railroad won several awards for public relations achievements, especially in advertising; and in politics he was such a familiar figure in Virginia legislative circles, deftly and skilfully wielding influence—if not downright power—on behalf of the railroad and its many causes that in time he became known as "the 41st Senator." His Cadillac's license tag number was an impressive 25. Small also served as Roanoke's mayor and it was largely through his pervasive and persuasive presence in local politics that the interests of the city and those of the railroad were widely thought to be virtually congruent, and possibly identical. "When the

railroad sneezes, Roanoke reaches for a handkerchief," a community saying for many years, was not altogether inaccurate, given the large number of railroad employees there.

Small recognized clearly that in Hotel Roanoke he had at hand not only a gleaming prize which reflected the railroad itself, but also a powerful hospitality-dispensing machine to which he had the key. When the railroad's inner circle discussed the Hotel and the talk turned to its financial support, his was undoubtedly the firmest voice in its favor, especially when it involved the million-dollar expansion in 1938 (and more to come in the years ahead).

Across the street from Small's office and easily visible from there was the imposing new facade housing Hyde and Denison, general manager and resident manager respectively. They constituted a team which until Hyde's death in 1963 relentlessly maintained and even enhanced Hotel Roanoke's standards of quality performance. Hyde had returned as general manager in 1938 as the new wing was being completed after an absence of three years. He had first come to the Hotel in 1928 as assistant manager; though he was only 21, he had already accumulated experience in the hospitality trade at a hotel in Winchester, Virginia. He was named manager in 1929 and resigned in 1935 to become manager of Richmond's John Marshall Hotel.

Kenneth Hyde

Hyde, darkly handsome, dedicated and charming, devoted much of his time to promotional matters and soliciting convention business for the new hotel. In an editorial tribute at the time of his death, the *Roanoke World-News* said "More than any other man, Ken Hyde made a science of obtaining conventions for the Star City...he played a tremendous part in keeping the city prosperous...Ken Hyde indeed filled the picture of the professional innkeeper...courtly, affable, polite, friendly in speech and attractive in manner. He was a credit to Roanoke and his passing is a sad loss to the community." It was a fine epitaph for the Hotel's manager.

He was also, according to Janet Jenkins, a religious man, who lived his faith at work. He was "...a fine gentleman, a devoted family man...who was concerned over the welfare of all Hotel Roanoke employees." He "enjoyed the respect and affection of all the hotel's managers and employees. I never heard a criticism of him." "A grand man" is the way Fred Walker, another Hyde subordinate and later a successor as the Hotel's general manager, described him.

Mrs. Jenkins went to work for the Hotel as a part-time secretary in 1950 and retired from it 30 years later as general manger, and so worked for Hyde for 13 years. "He was a strong taskmaster, but a kindly one—and so enthralled with the hotel business that he was sometimes oblivious to his surroundings." One day, early in her career, the secretarial staff decided to put this apparent detachment to a test.

"It was around Halloween and I had a Groucho Marx pair of glasses with mustache to take home. I bet the girls I could wear them into his office (for dictation) and he would never notice them. Well, it was a good fifteen to twenty minutes before he even looked at me. I could hear girlish giggles outside the door. When he did look, he was highly incensed and gave me a lecture on appropriate

Hotel Roanoke behavior in the office.

"Also, I was a great soft whistler. One day he came into my cubicle and quoted 'whistling girls and cackling hens will never come to any good end.' I apologized and desisted. Several weeks later he came into the cubicle again and said 'JJ, I miss your whistling.' So I laughed and resumed—and haven't stopped to this day."

Roaming the Hotel every day was a part of the gregarious Hyde's job, especially enjoyable because it provided the opportunity to talk to the staff at all levels. Occasionally, these tours bore fruit—literally. One former employee recalled that Hyde would sometimes stop in the kitchen, pick up a banana and eat it. "Charge it to Mr. Griffith," he would say with a smile and continue his rounds. (Griffith was the executive steward at the time.)

The outside view of the Hotel's general manager was essentially the same as the inside. As a journalist, John Eure had a continuing view of the man at work. "I saw Ken Hyde three or four times a week as a matter of course. He was accommodating and amiable, as he should have been to reporters; he had a good sense of public relations and what reporters wanted; but he was also a fine man."

Such was the man who assumed command of the "new" Hotel Roanoke. On hand when he returned to take up his new post was George Denison, a veteran of the hotel business. He had worked for a Florida hotel in 1925, briefly for Hotel Roanoke in 1927, then with a New York hotel and at the Hotel Chamberlin in Hampton, Virginia, before returning to Hotel Roanoke in 1930, there to stay

George Denison

Janet Jenkins, left, the "great lady" of the Hotel for many years, discusses convention bookings with Walter Chapman, catering manager, and Judy Walker, secretary

until his retirement as manager in 1964. During Hyde's three-year absence (1935-38), Denison served as manager. (When World War II came, history repeated itself: Hyde left for service with the Navy and Denison became manager. Upon Hyde's return after the war, they were designated co-managers.)

From 1938 on, at least in the last two or three years of peace before the world was irrevocably changed, Hotel Roanoke sailed on its serene way, polishing its success as assiduously as it did the handsome paneling in the Lobby. About the Hotel's staff, Fred Walker, general manager in the late 1960s, observed that they were "the salt of the earth. If the words 'loyal' and 'dedicated' can be used anywhere, they should describe these people. They all of them—dining room waiters, bellmen, room service waiters, maids, desk clerks, secretaries, dishwashers, cooks, sales people, most of them anonymous—did their jobs day by day, and did them well."

There were others too, less anonymous, who became part of the Hotel's legend, in one case through fame, in another through sheer longevity—and quality. In June 1942, J. Ed (Deacon) Brown, assistant headwaiter, completed an astonishing 60 years of service with the Hotel, and was honored by having his photograph on the front of the Dining Room menu.

Incredibly, he was still autographing them for patrons in early 1945. "He made quite a good thing out of signing those menus," recalled one who observed Brown in action, "because each autograph was usually good for a couple of dollars." (Food costs shown in that wartime menu reflected government-imposed price controls, but

even so, were remarkable. Two lamb chops, $.95. Peach Melba, $.30; the most expensive item was a planked steak for two, at $4.00.)

In honoring Deacon Brown's anniversary, the old gentleman—who might well have brought dinner to Frederick Kimball—was given two $50 Defense Bonds by Hyde and Denison in a Ballroom ceremony crowded with Brown's fellow employees. "I worked in the original wooden building when all we had was 38 rooms, with iron beds, hard chairs and bad lights. Now look at this place," he said. "It's the finest in the country." In his six decade-plus career, Brown served such luminaries as Charles Evans Hughes, William Jennings Bryan, J. P. Morgan (reportedly

> "He made quite a good thing out of signing those menus," recalled one who observed Brown in action, "because each autograph was usually good for a couple of dollars."

fond of the Hotel's scrambled eggs), and Mrs. Calvin Coolidge, and put his four children through college.

Not far behind was William Campbell, who in 1948 celebrated his 45th anniversary and for whom "a lifetime as a waiter" was synonymous with "a lifetime of happiness." When he started out in 1903, "the place was almost a log cabin. There was a porch all the way around the building and the only way you could get to the rooms was from that porch. Many is the time I've taken those steps two at a time to keep warm in winter." Like Deacon Brown, Campbell too sent all his children—four sons and two daughters—to college, and like him too, had his photograph on the front of a congratulatory menu.

To say that fame came to Fred Brown is less accurate than to say that fame came to Fred Brown's creation. For it was in 1940—when Deacon Brown had been a waiter for only 55 years, and two years after the Tudor entrance was installed—that Chef Brown invented Hotel Roanoke's signature Peanut Soup. Manager Hyde had been after Chef Brown to produce something new and different for the Hotel. Chef "kept on putting things together"—until after a long period of experimentation, during which he established ordinary peanut butter as the prime ingredient, he declared himself satisfied. Favorable reaction was immediate, as was the new soup's fame. Requests for the recipe came from all over the world, and for a time, Fred Walker recalls that the Hotel closely guarded the recipe and declined to share it. In the face of hundreds of requests every year "we finally printed it and sent it to anyone who asked. They had probably been our guests, after all." It has since been reprinted by the Hotel in its own promotional material and in many published cookbooks;

patient readers of this book will find it here as well.

Brown started with the Hotel on July 4, 1922, while he was still in high school. He was a "runner," fetching supplies from the storeroom to the kitchen, and after graduating from high school worked his way up on the food preparation side: "boiler cook, fry cook, then roast cook, then assistant chef—grand marche—that's the cold meat cook," he told Ann Fox Sprague, a writer for the *Norfolk and Western Magazine* at the time of his retirement in May 1964. In 1927, he left the Hotel to improve his trade elsewhere as assistant chef or chef. But like so many others, including Denison, Hyde and Warren Webb, he found the lure of the old place irresistible. So after grazing in other pastures, notably the Greenbrier Hotel, he returned to his beloved Hotel Roanoke as executive chef in 1937. Good humored, he was, and a perfectionist, but not temperamental—except once, according to Warren Webb, who was steward at the time. In a moment of uncharacteristic irascibility following a dispute with another employee, Brown ran him out of his kitchen with such energy that he lost his false teeth.

Sprague has recalled being invited to lunch with Chef at his own table in the kitchen, a rare privilege for an outsider. From that table after planning discussions with Lee Griffith, the Hotel's executive steward (and predecessor of Warren Webb), came the dishes and specialities that delighted diners for many years. The continuing cuisine was not limited to "Southern"—peanut soup, of course, and country ham, fried chicken and chess pie, and all the traditional accustomed Dixie trappings. The menu listed seafoods (especially from Virginia), lamb, beef, salads, and all of the other items which kept diners returning time and again for memorable dining.

Griffith's Hotel Roanoke career began in 1930, and when he retired in May 1969—coincidentally the same day as Chef Brown—he was executive steward. He was responsible for buying all the food and beverages served from the kitchen and helping prepare the menus, and even had a hand in the design of the new kitchen for the 1938 remodeling.

Chef Brown, being the Chef, was always the star of Hotel Roanoke cuisine and king of the kitchen, but never more so than at Thanksgiving. It was perhaps the busiest day in the Hotel's year, at least during the 1950s and '60s. For that day, all the furniture was removed from the lobby both to protect it from and make room for the crowds attending the annual Virginia Military Institute—Virginia Polytechnic Institute football game in Roanoke,. VPI's headquarters were in the Hotel, VMI's in the Hotel

Hotel and union officers sign the agreement ending the 1983-84 six-month strike. From left, Hotel General Manager Peter Kipp and Union Secretary James Wade. In back, George Gardner, Hotel attorney, and Tom Kircher, union attorney

Patrick Henry. Nobody got the day off. Hundreds of box lunches were put up in the big kitchen for the game attendees. One Thanksgiving 1,200 persons were served dinner, at the rate of three 30-pound turkeys for every 100 diners. The cranberry sauce was prepared personally by Joe Brown, the assistant chef who in time succeeded Fred Brown. Joe Brown (no relation to Fred) served in the Navy during the Second World War, working in his ship's galley and serving in a gun crew as well.

If Chef Brown was the undisputed king behind the swinging doors, the Regency Room itself had its own monarch, in fact two. These were Charles Hofer, maitre d'hotel and his assistant, Joseph Brenneis, whose European training added a cosmopolitan counterpoint to the warm Southerness of Hotel Roanoke. Hofer's unflappability was sorely tested in the Regency Room one night. He was escorting a Roanoke matron of some standing to her dinner table when her stride faltered perceptibly. Turning, Hofer observed what the woman already knew, that her panties had fallen to her ankles. The two carried off the incident with great *savoir faire,* the woman carefully stepping out of the garment, Hofer coolly pocketing it and both continuing on to the table. After dinner, the woman retrieved it from Hofer, who had carefully put it away in his desk. "A classic example of style," was the way the incident was described by the manager who later recounted the anecdote.

Hofer and Breneiss were natives of Vienna and served their apprenticeship in that city's Hotel Metropole. Friends, they worked separately in Paris, London, Geneva and the Riviera, and were reunited in Holland. The pair moved to the United States in 1927 and worked in sever-

The Regency Room in the late 1940s

al U. S. cities. Hofer came to the Hotel Roanoke in 1932, Breneiss in 1938. Duties consisted of arranging for all of the banquet activities in the Hotel, not just the routine meals of the area's various service clubs which regularly met there, but the large scale meals—breakfasts, luncheons, and dinners associated with the conventions.

In their time and later, when 150 conventions each year were commonplace, much of the banquet activity was in the Crystal Ballroom. It could accommodate over a thousand at a meeting, 900 for meals and 600 for dinner dances. Sometimes, all three events were held consecutively on the same day. Billy Davis and Alphonso "Alex" Alexander, banquet managers after Hofer and Breneiss's time, still boast of the efficient turnaround they achieved with their staff when a black tie cattle auction in the

Crystal Ballroom in the 1960s was followed by a Roanoke Symphony Ball that same night. A VPI student told a reporter afterward that "it was purely different, leading a Hereford on sawdust under chandeliers." The sawdust was spread over rubber mats to protect the floor during the auction. Billy Davis recalled later that the lingering aroma after the auction was noticeable, but with the aid of "maybe hundreds of spray cans of deodorizers, we cleared it out quickly" to set the room up for the Ball a few hours later.

Billy Davis and "Alex" Alexander were for many years so omnipresent at the Hotel's social events that they became virtually interchangeable parts of the mechanism. Davis started working in the Dining Room while he was still a high school student in 1943; Alexander began as a hall

Billy Davis and "Alex" Alexander prepare for a reception

boy in 1947. They both retired when the Hotel closed in 1989, Davis as banquet manager, Alexander as his assistant. They were trained in Hotel service, as they trained others, in a "hand-me-down" fashion–which is not to be taken to mean shabby or worn-out. It meant teaching new employees the style and quality that was a part of the Hotel way of doing business. "Old-timers taught us that quality begins at the front door," said Davis; "we taught the same lesson to new ones." Their work hours stretched endlessly across the clock, often from early in the morning to well after midnight, because "if there was an event going on, one of us was always there," Alexander said. These two men, dignified, able, courteous, epitomized the character of Hotel Roanoke to the very end. They not only passed on the tradition–they were part of it.

The heart of the Hotel's food and banquet service began, of course, in the huge kitchen. Typically, the Hotel's cooks arrived for work at 5:30 in the morning to prepare for the day. Cooks and waiters had their own jargon: scrambled eggs with visible white were "showing a little country;" eggs that were too runny required "tightening up." French toast was cut thick from an unsliced loaf. "Last night's un-ordered baked potatoes were this morning's hash-browns," according to Webb. A farmer from Franklin County would come in every day to pick up food scraps for his pigs; and every day he would faithfully return any silverware that had been inadvertently tossed out. After a while, this practice, useful though it was to man and beast alike, was stopped by health authorities.

The Saturday Night Buffet, in its time as compelling a tradition as the Sunday Brunch, was in later years a triumph of Southern cuisine. There was shrimp, steamboat round, ham, turkey, and fried chicken as the principal dishes, plus of course, the usual vegetables and desserts. All this was priced at $3.50, and in addition, there was dancing on a rather small floor in the middle of the Regency Room.

Years earlier Warren Webb, job-seeking at the Hotel, was told to come back when he turned 16 (in February 1944). This he did, deciding to stop at the Hotel that very day, a Saturday. He was hired on the spot by James Hunter, the assistant manager. "Start right away," he told young Webb, who protested that he was on his way to a movie. "You want a job or you want to go to a movie?" asked Hunter. Given such a stark choice, Webb picked the job. It paid him $100 a month and one meal a day. The Hotel at this time was housing Army Air Force and later Navy flying officers taking four weeks of wartime class work and flight instructions in DC3s at Roanoke's Woodrum Field. They and those with wives were housed in the south wing, and having turned over their food ration books—everybody had one during the war— to the Hotel, were fed in the Regency Room as residents. For their relaxation, the government took over the Pine Room to serve as an Officers Club. It was fitted out with a juke box playing what are today's Golden Oldies, a small dance floor, a bar, and even a guard usually the Officer of the Day—at the door. It was there that Warren Webb went to work, serving as bartender, setting up soft drinks and generally keeping the place clean. He worked at the Hotel for a while, then left, then as so many others did, finally came back to stay. He retired in 1985 after 25 years as purchasing and stores manager, responsible for the workings of the kitchen and storeroom.

Warren Webb, food and beverage manager, became busier than ever when Virginia amended its liquor laws

The various Parlors could accommodate meetings, parties and poker amd bridge games, or in this case, dinner

In its own way, the Officers Club contributed to Roanoke's social life. The same Helen Fitzpatrick who recalled her parents dressing in costume for the German Club, likewise remembered USO dances at the Hotel for its resident flyers, the Navy men "so handsome in their dress whites." Bachelor officers would find dates at Hollins College or elsewhere in the area, much as the German Club members did in the early days. One officer was married to Gail Patrick, a popular movie star of the time, who later had a kick-off role in the city's United Fund campaign one year. She was "a lovely person, and much in demand at community functions."

Another "name" visitor to the Officers Club was Morton Downey, who in 1944 brought his orchestra to the Hotel and broadcast his regular national network radio program from the Crystal Ballroom. After the show he had a piano moved into the Pine Room and played for the officers and their guests until nearly two in the morning.

The war ended; Gail Patrick went back to Hollywood and relative obscurity, the officers and the Pine Room all returned to civilian life and the Hotel began to prepare for business in the postwar world. The smoke of battle had scarcely dissipated when at the end of September 1945, the Norfolk and Western announced another million-dollar facelift at the Hotel, compatible with the Hotel's Tudor style. The project involved mainly the replacement of the four-story wing parallel to the railroad tracks—the south wing— with one of five stories. New bedrooms raised the total to 361, and each room was equipped with on-the-wall radios with a choice of four radio stations. These rooms, incidentally, within sight

and sound of railroad operations, exerted an appeal which the architects—Smith, Small and Reeb, of Cleveland—could not have foreseen.

Arthur M. Bixby, a railroad enthusiast and historian, frequently called on the Norfolk and Western on behalf of Dresser Industries, a supplier of railroad equipment. Arriving in Roanoke in the morning from New York via NW No.1 from Hagerstown, he would find "a Hotel Roanoke porter with a two-wheel cart waiting on the platform beside the sleeper, who would take your luggage and wheel it up the hill to the Hotel. A 25-cent tip was big in those days...Most of the time a desk clerk named Skippy was on duty and assigned me a room on the track side of the Hotel, at my request. While going to sleep, I would listen to the soft chuff-chuffs of the Class Y compound mallets and the sharp barks of the single Class A 2-6-6-4s, identifying them by class from their sound." This ability to distinguish one steam locomotive from another by its sound, while astonishing to some, is not uncommon among knowledgeable rail fans. Dr. Raymond Smoot, later a vice president of Virginia Tech, has recalled that he could do it himself and would occasionally check into the Hotel for the sheer enjoyment it provided him as guest and rail fan. At least twice in subsequent years, the National Railway Historical Society held its annual meeting there, and the rooms facing the track were the first to be reserved.

Levels below the new guest rooms, the architects situated a row of small Parlors, each handsomely furnished and equipped with a marble—but non-working—fireplace. These rooms were designed for meetings and small conferences and could easily seat sixteen or eighteen guests

The model removes her gloves to switch on a guest room radio in this 1947 photograph

for sit-down meals; to accommodate more elaborate events and larger numbers, they could be opened into each other. A small group of senior railroad officers, led by President W. J. Jenks, would from time to time make evening use of three of the Parlors, one for cocktails, one for dinner, the third for poker.

The Fountain Room was new—a "modernistic and colorful gathering place" was the way it was described in the *Norfolk and Western Magazine*—with fluted marble columns supporting the ceiling, a seating capacity of 125 and murals showing Virginia scenes and historical events. Its menu was undemanding and satisfying and it filled a specific need in the Hotel for an eating place more intimate than the formal Regency Room. Just the same, in those days when "informal" meant something different than it came to mean in later years, most ladies lunching there came in hats and sometimes gloves.

Just as this addition brought the Fountain Room to life the next major work, in 1955, ended it. The Fountain Room, popular and attractive, had served its purpose, and was replaced by a seven-in-the-morning-to-ten-at-night Coffee Shop with a soda bar and seating for an additional 100 guests. Later, to meet the increasingly diverse tastes of its clientele, the Coffee Shop also disappeared, and the Hotel used the same space for the Windsor Room, the Ad Lib Club, offering food, drink and jazz and finally, Jimmy Butler's Comedy Club.

With the 1946-47 work, Hotel Roanoke became completely air-conditioned, a circumstance somewhat at variance with the boast that in the 1938 rebuilding it had become the first hotel to be "scientifically designed for air-conditioning." It seems clear that being designed for cooling and being actually cooled were two different things. In any event, the project also included a major kitchen expansion, adding walk-in refrigerators capable of holding a thousand steaks, and separate kitchen facilities for the Fountain Room. A Turkish bath was also installed. Work started in December 1945 and ended in early 1947, somewhat behind schedule.

Although there would be other guest services instituted—the motel entrance, the swimming pool, a convention exhibition-hall, re-decorating, attractive watering holes for thirsty conventioneers, there was only one more major construction project to come before the Hotel was closed in 1989. Costing $1.2 million and opening for business in March 1955, a new five-story-and-basement north wing parallel to Jefferson Street added 56 guest rooms, the Shenandoah Room for conventions, the Coffee Shop mentioned above, expanded kitchen space and an employee cafeteria.

Vice President Sydney Small underlined the significance of this "costly addition" when he noted that it was made primarily to accommodate increasing demands for larger convention facilities. The Hotel clearly felt that whereas guests and their families would always be welcome and cosseted with Hotel Roanoke's trademark service and hospitality and would not be ignored, the nation's changing business mores had created a burgeoning convention trade. An investment to meet these increasingly sophisticated and diverse demands would surely bring a return—and, one hoped, a substantial one. The number always to be watched and improved upon was the occupancy rate.

Top: the Hotel around 1950 in an extensively retouched photograph; lower left, a typical '60s family relaxes in their room; lower right, the living room of the penthouse apartment in 1938

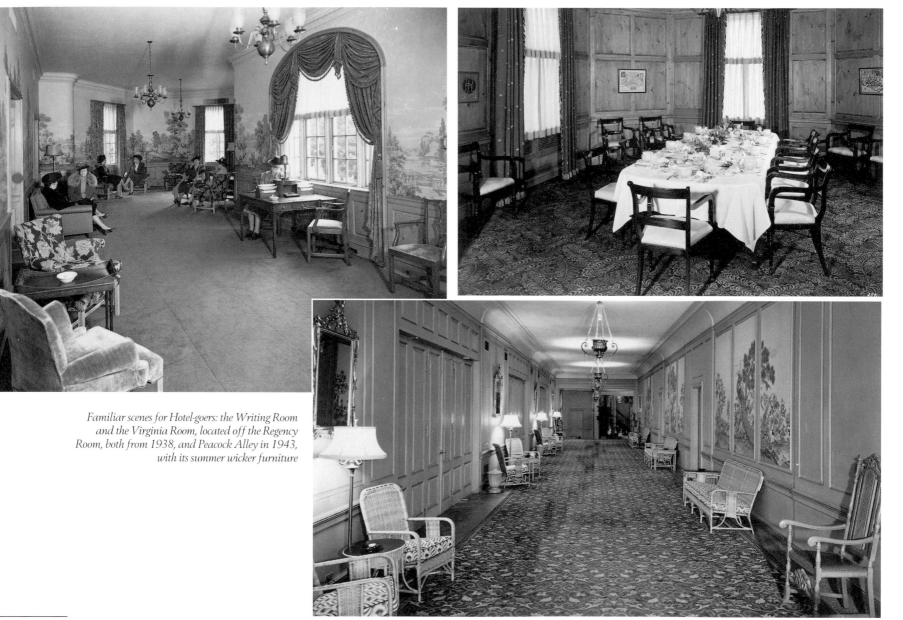

Familiar scenes for Hotel-goers: the Writing Room and the Virginia Room, located off the Regency Room, both from 1938, and Peacock Alley in 1943, with its summer wicker furniture

CHAPTER III

Filling The House

The convention trade had been part of the Hotel's business from its very beginnings. It was not a year old when in June 1883 the American Institute of Mining Engineers met there. The aim then—to put guests in the rooms and diners at the tables— was the same in 1952. In the new postwar business climate the Hotel produced and distributed widely a film called "Hospitality Unlimited." It was directed principally at the convention/business meeting market, and showed off the Hotel and its many guest services—although sometimes straining the putative "story line" to do so.

For example, when breakfast is brought to one of the film's stars (an opportunity to show off a wheeled cart with a built-in warming unit) and manages to spill coffee on his shirt through a gap in the front of the handsome dressing gown—far too upscale a garment to be called a bathrobe— he is wearing. The reason he spilled the coffee was that he was using the cup as a baton keeping time to the music coming from the four-station wall radio he had just turned on. No problem, says the narrator; Hotel Roanoke has a modern laundry to take care of just such mishaps. The laundry is then shown, along with an "ingenious machine" to sew on buttons.

"Hospitality Unlimited" has at this distance a dated charm:

the men all in suits and ties, even when driving along the Parkway in an immense top-down convertible. In the opening scene, Hotel guests arrive on a passenger train hauled by a Norfolk and Western Class J locomotive. The women detrain wearing hats, gloves and furs.

Bellmen escort the guests to their rooms and point out the new amenities: "turn a knob and the weather is at your command," and the "individually wrapped drinking glasses." When the guests order dinner, the film has an opportunity to show the "exclusive dogwood pattern china," kitchen facilities, huge food lockers, the bake shop and even a machine that manufactures ice "never touched by human hands." After dinner, one of the men offers cigarettes around his table. The waiter offers a light, "a little touch that makes a difference," says the film's narrator.

While the business sessions go on, the women are manicured in the Beauty Shop, play bridge in the Pine Room and

Guests at the main entrance in 1949

prepare postcards "for the folks back home in the Writing Room." Some of the men, possibly skipping the business session, are in the Barber Shop or the adjacent Health Club. One, in shirt and tie, is working out on a stationary bicycle; another, presumably *not* wearing a shirt and tie, is in the steam bath, and a third is getting a rubdown. The film ends with the Executive Committee of the organization holding its meeting at the Hotel approving the motion that "we meet here again next year."

A second film, produced in 1963, shows off new facilities and conveniences installed after "Hospitality Unlimited" was made. There were little things, such as television sets in the rooms and message lights on the telephone; but there were major additions designed with the business meeting clientele in mind. These included the Shenandoah Room, Exhibit Hall, fitted out to handle large displays, the Motor Inn and for the conventioneers, overnight guests and towns-folk as well, the new (in 1962) swimming pool, and the noon snacks and evening dancing around it. This film, nar-rated by the late Robert Porterfield, the man who put Abingdon's Barter Theater on the map, ended with the same happy messsage as the first film: "my group voted to come back next year."

Nineteen-sixty-three was the year Ken Hyde died and was succeeded as general manager by George Denison. When, slightly more than a year later, Denison himself retired, he turned the Hotel over to a bright, energetic team, headed by Carl G. Thurston. Thurston, a Roanoke native and a career hotel man, returned to his hometown to fulfill a dream of many years. When he heard the call from Hotel Roanoke he was manager of the Hilton Hawaiian Village, at that time the world's largest resort hotel. He had also been man-

ager of the Waldorf-Astoria Hotel in New York. Another member of the new management team was Fred Walker, also a Virginian, who had come to the Hotel as director of sales from the Hotel Chamberlin in Hampton, Virginia, and who would in time become general manager himself. With them in the front office and providing continuity with the past was Janet Jenkins who, having come to the Hotel in 1950 as a part-time secretary, became its general manager in 1976. It was she who has described the major players of the time: Denison was "a cultured gentleman who never lost his temper," Thurston, "a man of almost aristocratic bearing, with many ideas and a great flair for promotion," and Walker, "outgoing and generous with his time." Still to come was Ken Wilkey, brilliant and innova-tive, who followed Walker as general manager in 1971. All of these, in their own way and following their own skills and talents, like their predecessors and successors, left memorable marks on thc Hotel and its image.

The Motor Inn was Walker's idea, and its addition to the Hotel, like Thurston's swimming pool, was virtually obliga-tory if the Hotel was to remain competitive. Just as it could be argued that the interstate highway system played a big part in the demise of railway passenger business, it can be argued with equal cogency that it didn't do much to help downtown hotels either. Hotel Roanoke caught it both ways. In the battle between trains and Interstates, the I's clearly had it.

In this connection, the observations of George Ruff, who saw the victory, are instructive. In the 1950s, he was Norfolk and Western's traveling passenger agent, a job title now as antique as "cordwainer." He was based in Memphis, and covered Tennessee, Arkansas, Texas, Oklahoma, New

Thurston, a Roanoke native and a career hotel man, returned to his hometown to fulfill a dream of many years.

Managers at work: upper left, Fred Walker with Carolyn Eddy, Miss Virginia 1964, left, and Vicki Sharon Nuckols, Miss Williamsburg, 1964; left, Carl Thurston, left, greets the Hotel's 3 millionth guest, Charles Zoppa of Richmond (1963). Skippy Epperly, veteran desk clerk, is in the middle; above, Ken Wilkey shows off the new (1963) Whistle Stop, the Hotel's highly successful watering hole

Mexico and Arizona. One part of his job was to solicit business and associations to plan their meetings and conventions at Hotel Roanoke, and while they were at it, to route themselves over Norfolk and Western tracks to get there. In many cases, the people he dealt with had memories of happy times spent at the Hotel, and this, he wrote later, "provided a great entree for a presentation." Such presentations frequently turned out to be profitable, as when one customer chartered a train to Roanoke and its Hotel. The president of a banking association in a western state routed his special train over NW tracks whenever possible; a traffic officer of a grain company wanted the pattern number and producer of the Hotel's distinctive dogwood china for his wife. Ruff later wrote, almost in amazement, that "it was difficult to understand how so many people in widely diverse parts of the country far removed from Roanoke could be so familiar with the Hotel."

Another source of potential passenger traffic—and Hotel occupancy—was the flow of students to and from Virginia's colleges and universities, especially those reasonably close to Roanoke: Roanoke College, Hollins College, Radford University, Longwood College (both known by other names in the days of which Ruff speaks), Virginia Tech, Washington and Lee University, Virginia Military Institute, Sweetbriar College, Randolph-Macon Woman's College, among others. Ruff got the names and addresses of new and returning students from the colleges' admissions

The Motor Inn, located in the east wing, opened in 1963. It was not a success and in due course, closed

offices, and so equipped, found it easy to suggest to the parents that they deliver their children to college personally, and while they're in the neighborhood, why, just stay at the Hotel Roanoke for a couple of days before taking NW's No. 3 west and home. Ruff discovered that often one parent or the other had a connection of some sort with their sons' and daughters' schools and already felt strong ties to them—and the Hotel.

Then after a bit, things changed, for the very people who formerly piled aboard a train and checked their trunks, golf clubs and tennis racquets ahead now found it easier and cheaper to load it all in a station wagon, somehow insert the student and maybe a sibling or two and spend a couple of

Two billboards, the top from 1938, proclaims the Hotel's new air conditioned status; the second is from a few years earlier, possibly the late 1920s

Once, in the 1960s, a livestock association staged a cattle auction in the Ballroom (the floor of which was suitably protected); in a very few hours, the same space was cleaned, deodorized and set up for a Roanoke Symphony Ball

nights en route at the proliferating motels. By then, these multi-storied buildings with their casual dining rooms, perhaps a bar, free breakfast, or at least free coffee and doughnuts, swimming pools, individual private room entrances with parking spots right in front, had come a long way from earlier "tourist courts" and "tourist cabins" of dreary appearance and even drearier repute. Why, reasoned the driver of a car loaded with children and luggage, should we drive downtown looking for a hotel when we had just passed a sign that read "Holiday Inn—Next Exit"? For many, these go-to-college, return-from-college expeditions took on the air of an enjoyable little family vacation.

So the traveling public not only got off the trains, they checked out of the downtown hotels as well. Even Hotel Roanoke, with a solid convention business and a small but solid core of patrons, was not immune from the general exodus. The Hotel tried to recapture some of its lost trade by borrowing the fundamental convenience appeal of its highway-side competition and wedding it to its own traditions of comfort and excellence. Thus in creating a Motor Inn in 1963, the Hotel was in fact following a national trend. *The Hospitality Industry in the United States* (Paul R. Dittmer and Gerald G. Griffin, Van Nostrand Reinhold, 1993) noted that "established center-city hotels, many of them near disused railroad terminals...were becoming ever more costly to maintain....Most were threatened with loss of business to the new booming motel industry... Many... began to call themselves motor hotels or motor inns to suggest that the automobile traveler would be as satisfied in these accommodations as he was in a motel."

Hotel Roanoke's Motor Inn was set up with its own desk staff in the wing on the northeast side facing the railroad's

Roanoke Shops. A new entrance was created, with its own canopy—which echoed the spirit but not the substance of the awning at the Hotel's main entrance on the other side of the sprawling building. It extended down the stairway that led to a parking spot for registering guests.

Alas, though Denison had proclaimed that "guests will be afforded all the convenience of a motel combined with the charm and comfort of a major hostelry," the Motor Inn's appeal was not large and its patronage less, especially in view of the slick motel competition in the Valley. Further, it was expensive to operate, because it required three desk shifts each day, a cost not supported by revenue. It turned out to be a failed experiment, limped along for a few short years, then with significantly less fanfare than attended its opening, quietly went out of businesss in the mid-1960s.

Such changes and improvements, steady and costly, were undertaken to make the Hotel, along with its ambiance, cuisine and other trappings, more attractive, especially to business meetings. Soliciting and landing such business was traditionally the prime concern of the Hotel's general managers. From Ken Hyde and George Denison, through Carl Thurston, Fred Walker, Ken Wilkey, Janet Jenkins, Peter Kipp and Doreen Hamilton Fishwick, each lent a particular talent and even genius to the goal of expanding the occupancy rate and filling the Regency Room. Hotel Roanoke thought its best convention market lay within a day's drive—in Virginia first, then neighboring states and then the remaining mid-Atlantic states. Such national conventions which came its way were mainly the outgrowth of local or regional organizations with national ties.

The convention business was eminently worth pursuing.

One of the Hotel's regular big events was the Norfolk and Western Railway's Annual Better Service Conference. These are the attendees at the 1952 meeting

The International Association of Convention and Visitors Bureaus reported that in 1987, just two years before the Hotel closed, there had been nearly 200,000 business meetings nationally, attended by 68.4 million persons, who spent $37.5 billion in the process. It was a large cash melon to dip a spoon into, and explains why Hotel Roanoke management devoted much of its energy to it. When Janet Jenkins retired as general manager in 1980, she had firmly or tentatively booked coventions as far ahead as 1990. When the Hotel closed, one of the terminal chores was to cancel meetings scheduled well into the '90s.

Sales and promotional efforts, including the films, personal calls by the Hotel staff in cooperation with an energetic group in the Roanoke Chamber of Commerce became highly successful. Some organizations never met anywhere else but the Hotel, and others returned if not annually then at least on a regular schedule. The Virginia Pharmaceutical Association came every two or three years. Robert A. Garland, a long-time Association member and a former Roanoke City Councilman, has said that the VPA's membership "felt that the Hotel Roanoke was far superior to its competition in other parts of the state and preferred it." He attended these meetings both as a member and as a child, when his father, a pharmacist, would bring him along.

The Virginias-Carolinas Hospital Association was another regular in the Hotel. It was always the biggest, counting up to 1,200 attendees. Though the Hotel could not accommodate that many guests—other city hotels took the overflow—Hotel Roanoke was the site of the business sessions and exhibits. It may be, of course, that films and sales talk persuaded such institutions to come to the Hotel, but it seems clear that what brought them back time and again was the Hotel itself, its facilities, style, service, menu and above all people.

An outstanding example of the Hotel's appeal is the experience of Moore's, the nine-state building materials chain. It held its first sales meeting in the Hotel in 1987, the second in 1988, the third in 1989 and had scheduled its fourth for 1990. The company came back because, in the words of Jim Boutilier, Moore's vice president-Human Resources, "they (the Hotel) have what we need," and cited events in the 1988 meeting. That year Moore's, bringing in 350 people from 75 stores and headquarters, required registration facilities, a total of six meals, plus two receptions, three refreshment breaks and two entertainment programs, each demanding its own lighting and sound needs, and of course, general meeting sessions and group seminars, plus of course, the appropriate number of guest rooms and suites.

Todd Sloboda, branch manager, speaks at Moore's 1989 Management Meeting in the Hotel

The problem, she explained, was that guests coming to the reception had to pass a display of caskets set up in Peacock Alley for a meeting of state morticians.

To accommodate all of this, which had been planned for months, Charlotte Facella, the Hotel's sale manager at the time, set aside the Ballroom and Shenandoah Room for the large meetings, meals, parties and entertainment. Half of the Exhibit Hall was devoted to signage, display materials and displays, and the other half had video games and pool tables for attendees' relaxation; the Core Room, tools and hardware; the Pocahontas-Cavalier Rooms, kitchen displays; the Pine Room, outdoor grills and lawnmowers, and the Oval Room, mini-computers and registration.

Each detail was written down long before the first chair was set up in the Ballroom, the first napkin folded in the Regency Room. Close connections among the Hotel's Departments—sales, catering, housekeeping, engineering, security—were absolutely essential. A coffee break ten minutes late, a burned-out bulb in a slide projector, a defective sound system could mean a spoiled meeting for the client and lost future business for the Hotel.

For Moore's "there (was) responsiveness and enthusiasm for our meeting," Boutilier has said. "And professionalism. I saw a lot of professionalism over there." Beyond the smooth running, beyond the high level of excellence, however, Moore's found a human side to the Hotel. "One of the men attending the (1988) meeting was in a major health situation, in need of a kidney transplant. We had told the Hotel staff about it; so when at 10:10 one morning we learned that a kidney had become available in Pennsylvania, the Hotel switchboard was able to locate our man and helped us charter a plane to take him to Pennsylvania. Another example: one of our blind employees was attending and for him, as for the kidney patient, the Hotel made special efforts. That's what I mean by professionalism, and nice

people. We had great experience at Hotel Roanoke."

Clearly, not all of Hotel Roanoke's meetings were as elaborate as Moore's, but many were larger. Five hundred attendees was an easily manageable number, which also left ample space for a smaller meeting or two as well as for individual guests.

An undated piece of puffery from the Hotel makes an interesting observation: "We serve approximately 175 conventions annnually—sometimes three at a time—and anyone attending all meetings there would have considerably more than a liberal education. He would learn about nursing, mathematics, metal health, railroad signals, candy merchandising, embalming, apple blight, sorority customs, maritime law and about every other item in the encyclopedia."

Conventions, whatever their content or size, were not always fully appreciated by other guests. On one occasion a woman who was holding her daughter's wedding reception in the Shenandoah Room at the end of Peacock Alley came to Billy Davis, the assistant banquet manager, in a highly upset condition. The problem, she explained, was that guests coming to the reception had to pass a display of caskets set up in Peacock Alley for a meeting of state morticians. It was all very upsetting and inappropriate on this happy occasion. Can something be done perhaps to remove them, she wanted to know. Alas, no ma'am, I am afraid not, was the courteous but unchangeable answer.

Weddings and receptions were a major part of locally generated business, involving, according to size, the Pine Room, the Shenandoah Room, and even the Ballroom for really

The Hotel and its grounds in the heart of downtown, before 1954

large parties. Billy Davis said he had handled so many weddings and receptions in his job as assistant banquet manager that he could virtually "cry on request." And yet, with all that, there was once even a funeral at the Hotel. Clearly not as joyful an occasion as the weddings, it nevertheless reflected the mystical, familial, personal hold the Hotel exerted on its guests.

Mrs. Ava Scott, a Roanoke music teacher, had retired and moved to Florida. Yet every year she would return to Roanoke and spend several weeks of the summer in the Hotel. One year she became very ill and had to return home to Florida, where she died. Her daughter told Janet Jenkins that Mrs. Scott, in her last years, had specified cremation and that her ashes be spread over the Hotel's grounds. After a review with appropriate city officials, this last guest request was granted. While Mrs. Scott's ashes were being scattered under a large magnolia on the Hotel's lawn by her daughter and a clergyman, Mrs. Jenkins was delivering a eulogy in Parlor D to a group of Mrs. Scott's friends. It was, she has said, "a touching and terrible experience, because I was very emotional."

Celebrating and grieving families aside, Hotel Roanoke had many allies in its steady efforts to fill the rooms. One was the railroad itself, which from the very beginning and by whatever name, enjoyed with the Hotel "a mutually advantageous arrangement," as one anonymous Hotel officer put it. The railroad's Board of Directors met there regularly, the Annual Shareholders' Meeting was held in the Crystal Ballroom (at which vast numbers of the Hotel's justly famous ham biscuits were consumed) and the special NW shareholders meeting in which the consolidation with Southern Railway was approved (in only four minutes) in the Shenandoah Room. Executives brought guests to lunch

and dinner. Among them was the Japanese ambassador to the United States, touring railroad facilities, for Japan was for many years the principal export destination for NW-hauled coal. William B. Bales, who later became the railroad's vice president for coal marketing, recalled that he was invited to lunch there by Vice President Thomas Hamill as part of Bales's job interview. "I was thoroughly impressed and my ego inflated considerably." In later years, "we had visitors from Japan and most countries in Europe and South America, and we always went to the Hotel for lunch or dinner. I would watch them taste peanut soup for the first time and sensed that they were not quite sure what they were eating—although everyone seemed to enjoy this special treat..." Lawrence Forbes, a former Virginian Railway officer and after that line's merger with the Norfolk and Western, one of Bales's predecessors as senior coal marketing officer, has a similar recollection: "I thought of the Hotel as a showplace for our foreign and domestic coal buyers. We always received raves about the grits and Virginia ham and peanut soup."

The railroad's principal and largest meeting in the Hotel for many years was the Annual Better Service Conference, requiring many of the Hotel's guest and meeting rooms for its sessions. This brought to the Hotel hundreds of employees from all levels for two or three days of earnest discussions on the paramount issue of providing Better Service to its customers. Various committees met for what are now called "break-out sessions" to hammer out ideas and suggestions and prepare reports. These were delivered in front of the entire group in the Crystal Ballroom.

It was here during the 1948 Conference that the late Richard F. Dunlap was required to deliver his committee's

Spring at Hotel Roanoke

The Hotel at twilight

The Lobby at the time of closing

ROANOKE, VA.

ROANOKE, VA.   Hotel Roanoke.

What do you think of this Hotel? It is supposed to be one of the prettiest in Virginia.

1061   HOTEL ROANOKE, ROANOKE, VA.

The Hotel as seen through postcards

Hotel Roanoke. Roanoke, Va.

Dear Nora, we miss you more & more every day. Here is a view. Hurry & come back Grandma

No. 82941 Van Lear Bros., Druggists, Roanoke, Va. (Germany)

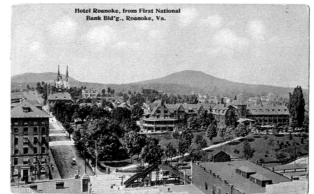

Hotel Roanoke, from First National
Bank Bld'g., Roanoke, Va.

Hotel Roanoke, Roanoke, Va.

Hotel Roanoke and Lawn, ROANOKE, Va.

21060

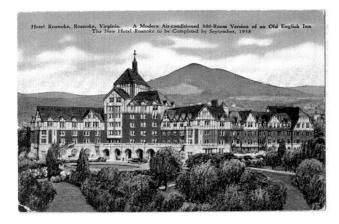

Hotel Roanoke, Roanoke, Virginia. A Modern Air-conditioned 300-Room Version of an Old English Inn
The New Hotel Roanoke to be Completed by September, 1938

KR-6 HOTEL ROANOKE AND OFFICE BUILDINGS OF NORFOLK AND WESTERN RAILWAY, ROANOKE, VA.

"PHOTO THRU COURTESY NORFOLK & WESTERN RAILWAY". 90542

R-57 HOTEL ROANOKE, ROANOKE, VA.

NIGHT VIEW OF HOTEL ROANOKE, ROANOKE, VA.—51

Hotel Roanoke, Roanoke, Virginia A Modern Air-Conditioned Version of an Old English Inn

COLOR PLATE 3

Indoor pool

*At right, two views of
Hotel Roanoke*

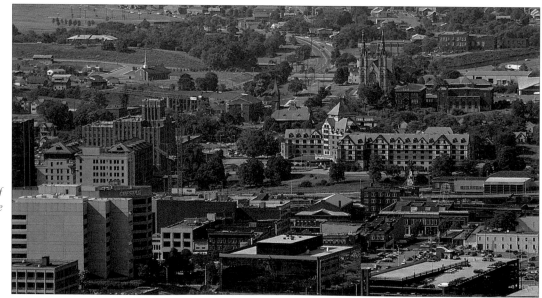

At left, Executive Chef Heinz Schlagel. Above, a Hotel employee prepares a guest room

Dinner and music in the Regency Room

Below, conviviality in the Whistle Stop

At right, last minute preparations in the Crystal Ball Room

Re-decorated guest room at the time of closing

The Regency Room, splendid and dignified, at the time of closing

Hotel employees at closing time are photographed

Dusk brought the touching final ceremonies. Rev. Noel C. Taylor, Mayor at the time, spoke movingly of the old Hotel; a Color Guard lowered the flag; and Doreen Hamilton Fishwick delivered the eulogy

Above, "Renew Roanoke" leaders toast their success. From left, Mayor David Bowers, former Mayor Noel C. Taylor, Thomas Robertson, and the late Dr. James McComas. At left, "Renew Roanoke" broadcasts its success live on Roanoke television.

report. Dunlap was a native Roanoker and recalled being taken at the age of ten to the Hotel after church for Sunday dinner. He had earned medals for valor and wounds as an infantry officer in New Guinea during World War II; in 1948, back on the railroad, he was assistant roadmaster in Crewe. He stood up to face not only 600 of his fellow railroaders, but President R. H. Smith, a formidable presence, as well. Recalling the incident 45 years later, he said "My knees were knocking, and I was sweating from armpit to belt buckle. I knew if I messed this up, I would be an assistant roadmaster for life." Since he subsequently became the Norfolk and Western's president in the course of a career in which timidity was conspicuously absent, readers may safely assume he did not "mess up" his report.

The railroad was also a major tenant at one time. It occurred shortly after the failure of the Motor Inn experiment, when the railroad was in the process of bringing new life into its piggyback, or intermodal, section, which then as now involved the movement of highway trailers and containers on railroad flat cars. To develop and exploit this promising line of business, R. B. Short—"Reggie" to all, "Shorty" to some—was brought in from St. Louis where this certified original had worked for the old Wabash Railroad. In Roanoke he found that there was no room in the General Office Building for his growing department. He looked at and rejected possible space in the railroad's garage behind the Hotel.

One day, late in 1967, along with Herman Pevler, Norfolk and Western's president (for whom Short had worked on the Wabash), and Richard Dunlap, then NW's vice president for operations, Reggie toured the former—and now empty—Motor Inn space. As Short recalls, the dialogue on

At work in the new kitchen, 1938

Miss Virginia notes: Mary Lou Bloxom, Miss Williamsburg, fits a colonial tricorn on the late Jack Smith at the 1970 pageant. As operating head of the Roanoke Regional Chamber of Commerce Smith did much to make the Miss Virginia pageant a major attraction to Roanoke – and the Hotel; Kylene Barker, the only Miss Virginia to become Miss America, was honored in 1978 when the Hotel hung her portrait in Peacock Alley. Miss Barker, holding flowers, seems pleased. Miss Virginia contestants of 1982 pose for their formal group photograph in the Oval Room

the tour ran roughly like this:

Pevler: "How would this do?"

Short: "Looks perfect."

Pevler (to Dunlap): "Draw up the plans."

The plans, when drawn and executed, called for tearing out some walls and fixtures to create space sufficiently large to accommodate Short's 40 intermodalists. They kept the Motor Inn canopy and had to themselves the entire first floor, which Larry Keoughan, one of the flock, remembered later as having none of the distractions found elsewhere, – meaning drop-in visits – and was thus "most conducive to working."

Reggie Short had a friend build for him a down-sized version of a highway trailer's back door and had it installed as the entrance to his department's offices.

What befell Hotel Roanoke's traditional decor after that has been described by Frank Wilner, a Short underling at the time (later a vice president of the Association of American Railroads), and who has referred to him as a "mercurial marketing magician."

"This [the trailer door]," he wrote, "was not sufficient to the decorating needs of Mr. Short. He demanded of each of his employees the attitude of a hungry tiger. So he ordered that the walls of his Intermodal Department be painted a burnt orange! And they were. And for months afterward, most employees left their daily labors with splitting headaches from the abusive glare that instigated not a few verbal arguments…"

Without apology—in fact, with something approaching pride—Short has cheerfully defended his decorating taste: his department's space was widely known as "Shorty's pumpkin." "In any case, we had good fun over there. We had good people. We were close to the Regency Room and the Pickwick Club and that impressed customers. We stayed busy taking customers away from the Chessie and the Pennsy. We made a few bucks, too."

And spent them. As tenants, even though railroad tenants, Short's department paid rent, which included, it should be noted, fresh-wrapped soap supplied by maid service every night. Janet Jenkins quotes fondly the Hotel's traditional rule: "there are no freebies. The NW pays its way, but it knows it's getting its money's worth in service." Even fresh-wrapped soap.

The railroad's presidents were frequent visitors. Or not, according to Mrs. Jenkins, who saw several of them. R. H. "Race Horse" Smith was a fairly infrequent visitor. He "ran in like a race horse to see Mr. Denison from time to time." Although she saw him on those occasions, he had no small talk beyond a "good morning." W. J. Jenks had lunch at the Hotel every day, and was served for dessert very thin cookies, made only for him and him alone. Stuart Saunders, founder of the modern merger movement among American railroads, would sometimes arrive "followed by a small retinue," and declare he wanted a meeting room right away. Some one would make faces at me over his shoulder in an attempt to make me laugh," she recalls. And did she? "Not that I recall."

Herman Pevler was "a great and good friend." When his election to the railroad's presidency was announced, the

Pickwick Club logo

newspaper published a photograph showing his shock of white hair. Soon after a man came in, wearing a hat, asking to see Fred Walker, the manager. "And whom shall I say..." began Mrs. Jenkins. "Pevler," he growled, and removed his hat to provide further identification.

When in April 1970 Pevler retired as president, he took office space in the Hotel on the floor just above the executive offices. Sharing the three-room suite with him were Jesse Gearhart, who had been on the presidential staff, and later Fred Walker, who had moved from the Hotel's general managership to become public affairs director of the Virginia Holding Company, another NW subsidiary. After Pevler's death, his widow told Mrs. Jenkins that he had wanted her to have his old desk, the same one, Gearhart believes, he had used as president of the Wabash Railroad. (Eventually the desk ended up in the Norfolk office of the chairman of Norfolk Southern Corporation, David R. Goode.)

Close behind the railroad itself as a major source of business was the Chamber of Commerce and its offspring, the Roanoke Valley Convention and Visitors Bureau. The dynamic Jack Smith, who headed the Chamber for many years, roamed far over the Commonwealth, sometimes accompanied by Fred Walker, talking to organizations about meeting at Hotel Roanoke, and often delivering his sales pitch directly to sitting conventions. Working with him on this ongoing effort were Jack Goodykoontz, John Kelley and Margaret Baker, making up what Janet Jenkins has called "a great team." "They knew that the city would share in whatever prosperity Hotel Roanoke enjoyed." Elizabeth Bowles, though not an official of the Chamber, and the Chamber's Smith and Mrs. Baker were major players in the

association of the Miss Virginia pageant with Hotel Roanoke, in bringing it to the Hotel, and in keeping it there. Mrs. Bowles as a member of Roanoke's Junior Woman's Club helped to obtain for Roanoke the available Miss Virginia franchise from the Miss America Pageant's famous Leonore Slaughter, beginning in 1953. A decade later, faced with the possible loss of the franchise, the ubiquitous Smith formed a non-profit organization (Miss Virginia Pageant, Inc.) to retain it for the Hotel and city. Directors were Horace Fitzpatrick, Robert Lynn, Barton Morris, John Butler, Richard Edwards and the Hotel's own Fred Walker.

The actual pageant ceremonies were held in other places in the city, but the Hotel became the pageant's headquarters, and the substantial business it brought in was especially welcome since it took place typically in July, the slow season. The house was filled with the contestants and accompanying chaperones (only their rooms were complimentary), families, friends, sponsors, volunteers and media folk. The pageant for many years was a major community event, with a parade and bands and the contestants in long dresses and gloves riding along perched on the back seats of new convertibles, provided by Roanoke's auto dealers.

Each new Miss Virginia had the use of a suite in the Hotel for the year of her celebrity. Kylene Barker, the only Miss Virginia (1978) to go on to become Miss America, got a further special distinction from the Hotel—a suite bearing her name. (It had been the John Randolph Suite, and a less likely pairing of the beauty queen and the irascible Virginian cannot be imagined. He was hot-tempered and a formidable hater. He once thrashed a fellow Congressman with his cane and compared another to a dead mackerel in the moonlight: "brillant but stinking.") Ms. Barker has

...a parade and bands and the contestants in long dresses and gloves riding along perched on the back seats of new convertibles...

declared that the Hotel "changed my life. It was the grandest hotel I'd ever seen...a quiet elegance that was hard to find elsewhere... (As Miss America) I had the opportunity... to stay in the most beautiful hotels, but hardly any of them could hold a candle to Hotel Roanoke."

She wrote a book, *Southern Beauty*, in 1984. "Even though it was a book to promote good diet, exercise, etc., I couldn't help but include the Hotel's recipe for Peanut Soup." *People*

The annual Chamber of Commerce dinner meeting (undated) was another regular event at the Hotel

Magazine's critic didn't like the book, she says "but loved the recipe."

Through the pageant the city and the Hotel derived considerable publicity, with well-known judges (one of whom thought spoonbread was a dessert). Every one of the Hotel's

managers, Margaret Baker, who worked with them all from the mid-1950s, reports, "was delighted to have the pageant. Doreen Hamilton Fishwick was especially good to us. Whatever we needed—within reason, anyway—she did for us. She said more than once that the pageant is good for us, for you, and the whole valley."

Taking the same line was Mrs. Bowles, who later served on Roanoke City Council. "The pageant brought us notice and prestige, since localities with contestants sent their own reporters; and in later years, the pageant was televised state-wide." She recalls that after the pageant, there was always a big party in the Ballroom for the sponsors, volunteers and contributors; but "under the rules in those days, the competitors couldn't be in attendance at parties where alcohol was served, so we arranged for them to have pizza parties in the Pine Room."

(Mrs. Bowles also had a personal part in bringing another sort of group to the Hotel, the reunion of the 106th Infantry Division, in which her husband served in the Second World War. At the Division's reunion in South Carolina in 1993, many asked when they would come back to "that grand Hotel." She also had a hand in bringing a state convention of ex-prisoners of war to the Hotel.)

For Misses Virginia, Hotel Roanoke was so much of a part of their lives that Margaret Baker says, one former titleholder returned to Roanoke for a visit and when she saw the Hotel was closed, "burst into tears."

The Chamber itself used the Hotel facilities—for out-of-town guests, for seminars and meetings and, most notably, its annual dinner meeting. Michael Ramsey, at the time a staff member, attended the 1981 meeting, his first black-tie event in Roanoke.

"Actually, only those of us on the dais wore black ties; the mostly male audience was in business attire, some obviously selected by their wives. The ambiance was inspiring...the chicken cordon bleu, a house wine not too disagreeable. I was impressed by how easily Billy and Alex seemed to orchestrate the staff without much of a fuss."

At a later dinner, the Chamber's membership-raising arm, the Backbone Club, was relegated to the Pine Room for lack of space in the Ballroom and had to watch the proceedings there on closed circuit television. Says Ramsey: "The Backboners were more exuberant than usual. It was a 'spirited' evening; the food-to-liquid ratio changing appreciably during the meal...The dessert was a banquet concoction topped with dollops of hard meringue which it was learned could be flung a far distance when propelled by a dessert spoon...That was the last time the Backbone Club was ever separated from the rest of the dinner guests."

The funds spent on the Hotel over the years increased its attractiveness to guests, not merely in the regular cycle of room re-decorating, but in facilities as well. Traditionally, the Hotel had provided good taste, elegance, even serenity, a combination Janet Jenkins has labeled "a little luxury for an economical price." As competition grew in the interstate highway/motel world, more was needed, simply because the traveling public—and the ever-growing size of the conventioning public—demanded it.

So there came the swimming pool in 1962, where Farnham's tulip garden had been planted nearly 35 years before. Later a roof made year-round swimming possible and Carl Thurston created a sun-and-fun club so Roanokers could enjoy the same relaxation as guests; even later there was also poolside meal service and night time dancing.

There was the Pickwick Club, a private eating-and-drinking establishment in the days before the state's liquor laws were changed to permit the sale of alcoholic beverages by the drink. It was handsomely furnished in a comfortable English style with period antiques, had its own kitchen and staff, separate from the Hotel in every respect but location. The Club also had the only working fireplace ever constructed in the Hotel (at least, since the "bar-rooms" in the original Hotel building); whimsical at best, it was seldom used. (One of its early managers kept his books on three-by-five index cards, a fact which created much bemusement on the part of one of the railroad's sophisticated financial officers.) Hotel guests were eligible for a membership which expired upon the guest's departure. The Pickwick Club made no money for the Hotel. When the Hotel eventually needed its space again, the Pickwickians voted to move elsewhere.

There was the Windsor Room, formerly the Coffee Shop, formerly the Fountain Room. "Proper but not stuffy," according to a Hotel publicity piece, its "good-time flair makes it one of Roanoke's most popular nightspots" for dinner and dancing and entertainment. Part of the entertainment was a jazz program on Sunday afternoons. Among the regulars was the Dave Figg Quartet (Dave Figg on tenor sax and his wife Gene on piano; Nat Thomas, bass, and Harry Jackson, drummer), "plus anybody who cared to sit in." These included Charlie Perkinson, who came to Roanoke in 1970 and soon developed a jazz following for his radio station, WPVR. He would tape the Sunday afternoon program for re-broadcast that same night from the station's studios in the Hotel. (On the station's staff at the time was Adrian Kronauer of "Good Morning Vietnam" renown.)

The Sunday programs typically started at three and went on two or three hours, and sometimes as late as 7:30, depending on who was playing and the level of the audience's enthusiasm. The attendance was generally good— "an eclectic group: college students, hotel guests, Roanokers black and white," Perkinson recalls. The Windsor Room later took up rock, and after a while, when interest dropped off, the Windsor Room too shut down.

There was the Ad Lib Club, Peter Kipp's idea for another jazz-and-food place to fill the same site. Done in glitzy red and black, Ad Lib attracted local musicians as well, plus big names from the jazz world: Teddy Wilson, the incomparable pianist who was one of the original members of the Benny Goodman Trio and Quartet, Maxine Sullivan, the singer, Charlie Byrd, jazz guitarist. Ad Lib was also open for lunch, though without the music. Briefly successful, its appeal eventually faded, the victim of a fickle public.

After its demise Jimmy Butler's Comedy Club in April 1988 settled in, and stayed until the Hotel closed. The club was open Wednesday—the night for local comic talent— through Saturday. Butler paid no rent, but took the gate to cover costs and profit, and also shared in some receipts. "Business was a ping pong ball," Butler says.

Ken Wilkey replaced Fred Walker as general manager and came with a sound expertise in the food and beverage side of the hotel business. He held a degree in hotel and restaurant management from Oklahoma State University and worked for the Sheraton Corporation, Ramada Inns, Inc., and General Hosts Corporation before coming to Roanoke. He has been described as "brilliant" by Janet Jenkins, and judging from two of his notable innovations in the Hotel, it is an accurate appraisal.

It was handsomely furnished in a comfortable English style with period antiques, had its own kitchen and staff...

Top, Tommy Gwaltney presides over a "preview opening" of the Hotel's Ad Lib Club in November 1987. The Club attracted a number of well-known jazz musicians in its all-too-short lifetime. Bottom, The Windsor Room, shown here in 1976, provided an eclectic mix of music; its Sunday afternoon concerts were taped and later broadcast

Almost immediately after his arrival in 1971, Wilkey set about adding a new style to the Regency Room. Working through Dodie Matze, a Roanoke pianist who occasionally provided music for the diners, Wilkey located and commissioned Joe Corne to create a trio for week end performances. Corne was a native North Carolinian, holding a master's degree in music from the University of North Carolina; a music teacher, he had also been state table tennis champion for many years and was nationally ranked. Corne came to Roanoke to join the city school system to teach orchestral stringed instruments, and incidentally to play with groups all over the Valley.

When the summons from Wilkey came, Corne already knew a sizable number of musicians from The Coffee Pot, a popular part of the Roanoke music scene, where they frequently played and where he taught them table tennis. With himself on bass, Ron Northrup, classically trained, on the piano, and Sherman Helms on drums, they auditioned and won the job and held it for an astonishing 17 years. The players varied over that time, drawn from a pool of talent assembled by Corne: pianists Bonnie Todenhoft, Ralph Gravely and Frankie Romano; basses Lennie Martin, Charlie Perkinson, Nat Paul Thomas, and Chuck Cooper, and drummers Morris Elam, Jimmy Lewis and Ronnie Law.

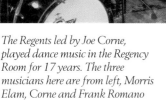

The Regents led by Joe Corne, played dance music in the Regency Room for 17 years. The three musicians here are from left, Morris Elam, Corne and Frank Romano

Corne recalls the Regency Room as "a place of glamour. The men were in tuxedos, the women in long dresses. Salads were fixed at the table, and eight dollars bought a first class dinner. The Windsor Room had excitement with its rock music, but the Regency Room had elegance."

On the first night, the trio themselves wore tuxedos. Although that was not every-night costume, Corne went through four during his playing years in the Regency Room. The room was full, and the trio began promptly at 7:00 P.M. with a resounding arpeggio from Northrup as an attention-getter, and then started in on their menu of show tunes, cocktail music and swing. So successful were they that after just a month or two Wilkey expanded their contract to include appearances seven nights a week. (It was not until they had been playing at the Hotel for seven years that they got around to naming themselves The Regents, and

that was "really just a joke," says Corne apologetically.

During breaks, Corne would often circulate through the dining room and chat with the patrons, making small talk and accepting requests for songs like the theme from "Dr. Zhivago," "Moon River," "The Way We Were," and "Send in the Clowns." One evening while roaming the room, he met the film star Donald O'Connor and talked with him about golf and entertainment.

The Regents' last night at the Hotel was November 27, 1989. Gravely, Law and Corne played the theme from "Love Story," a tune they had played on their first night 17 years before. "It was a beautiful night," Corne recalls.

The Regents had been playing for five years when Wilkey brought to life the Whistle Stop, an incredibly successful watering hole, serving drink and food in a determinedly railroad atmosphere, a bow to the Hotel's and city's origins.

At that time, Wilkey told the *Norfolk and Western Magazine* that "People seem to be very excited about it. The Hotel needed a place for people to eat that was quiet and moderately priced and this area has provided a happy medium." Wilkey himself undertook to collect much of the memorabilia which decorated the Stop. There were brake sticks, oil cans and shovels from old Norfolk and Western days, a collection of buttons from the uniforms of employees formerly in dining car service, an original poster from 1938 celebrating the railroad's 100th anniversary, lanterns, photographs, and a wrought iron window from the old Christiansburg passenger station's ticket office. As a finishing touch, a sound system was installed so that tapes of train noises could be played for patrons at regular intervals. The

Whistle Stop was popular (Senator Charles Robb recalled visiting there with friends for a nightcap) and busy for all its days and nights. Its assortment of railroad memorabilia lent a genuine railroad flavor to the place, which though lacking the cool elegance of the Regency Room, nevertheless remains a fond memory for thousands of Hotel guests. Like the Comedy Club, the Whistle Stop remained open to the very end, and after the Hotel closed, all of the railroad memorabilia passed to Norfolk Southern.

Opening day at the Hotel's pool in August 1962 attracted Roanoke Mayor Willis Anderson, left, and interested guests and bystanders, and, top, Patricia Jean Gaulding, the reigning Miss Virginia, and opening day swimmers

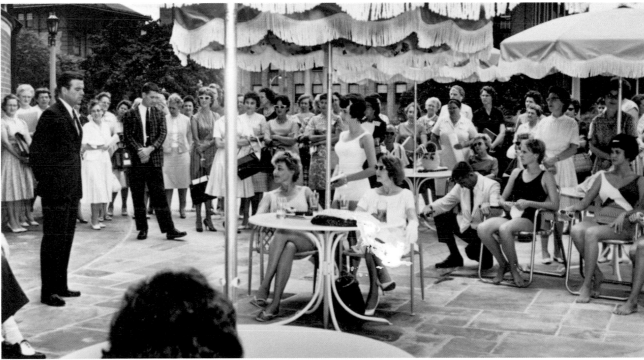

The backbone and strength of the Hotel, all its managers agree, resided in its personnel. This is a group of employees gathered in the early 1980s to celebrate their long service. Front row: unknown, unknown, Virginia Dickerson, Jean Powell, unknown, Marie Berry, J. Martin, L. Dent, unknown, unknown, unknown, unknown, unknown, K. Lawson. Back row: Billy Davis, Willie Hurt, Jr., "J.D.", Warren Webb, Pete Barnes, H. King, James Leftwich, Walter Knapp, "Shorty" Leftwich, General Manager Peter Kipp, who presented the service awards, Claude Minter, Mike Mason, Thema Goble

CHAPTER IV

Let Us Now Praise - Or At Least Talk About - Famous People

It is generally agreed that John D. Rockefeller–the original John D. Rockefeller–was once a guest of the Hotel–one wishes it to be so, of course. And if so, it raises interesting, if petty, questions. Did he tip the bellman and waiters a shiny dime? Did he pay his bill in shiny dimes? Was he even presented a bill?

Never mind; if he was a guest he was but one–albeit the richest–of many notables. There were Amelia Earhart and Joe DiMaggio, whose names have also been traditionally associated with the guest registry. Victor Borge and Ethel Merman and a Barrymore or two, and others can be considered to be likely, because of appearances at the famed and much-lamented Roanoke Academy of Music. Lawrence Tibbett, the great baritone from the Metropolitan Opera, however, is a sure thing, because John Eure, a Roanoke practicing journalist, interviewed him at dinner in the Regency Room on the night of his concert in the old Academy. (Confirming views held by old-line Roanokers, Tibbett told Eure that the Academy had the finest acoustics of any hall he had ever sung in.)

Another concert artist, the pianist Van Cliburn, years later made a lingering impression on the Hotel and its management. While practicing a few hours before his concert, he had left the water running in his bathtub, which ultimately overflowed and leaked through the Regency Room ceiling. No one was injured—the diners' peanut soup remained undiluted— but years later Janet Jenkins still didn't know, despite her instructions, how the piano got above the first floor.

A confirmed sighting is General Dwight D. Eisenhower, who was photographed with Mrs. Eisenhower leaving the Hotel—he with his trademark grin and she with a fussy little hat—after an overnight stop during his term as Army Chief of Staff.

Billy Sunday, the traditional fire-and-brimstone evangelist, stayed at the Hotel during a six-week crusade in Roanoke. "I have hoped," he declaimed, "for ten years that the Lord would let down the gates to Roanoke and let me in." He told a reporter in his Hotel Roanoke room that "I have preached in Norfolk, Richmond and Bristol and those experiences were just like a Smithfield ham—one taste and you want more." This was in September 1920, long before peanut soup appeared on the Regency Room menu.

Jack Dempsey and Jeanette MacDonald, an unlikely combination, are also recorded guests. The former had been in Roanoke to referee a wrestling match, and said of the place in which he spent the night, "That sure is a fine Hotel—one of the best in this part of the country," and spoke of its "remarkable service." Miss MacDonald, "looking very chic in a beige wool traveling frock, mink coat and felt hat trimmed with coq feathers," was in the city to sing a

> *"I have hoped,"he declaimed, "for ten years that the Lord would let down the gates to Roanoke and let me in."*

concert in the Roanoke auditorium, and stayed in a Hotel suite.

Helen Fitzpatrick, then a reporter, remembers during the war interviewing Carlos P. Romulo. He was in Roanoke on some now-forgotten mission, a refugee from the Philippines, an associate of General Douglas MacArthur before and during the war. "I was terrified, but he put me at ease, speaking of his family (still in the occupied Philippines) whom he had not heard from. I recall feeling so sad for him, as he did not know if they were dead or alive." (Romulo after the war became the Philippines ambassador to the United States.)

Philip Sporn, president of American Electric Power Company, meeting at the Hotel one year with his system's managers, had a serious complaint. A man whose intellectual capacity put him at the genius level, he was an inveterate reader; and that, stapled to his electrical background, made him unhappy when he discovered that there were no 100-watt light bulbs in his suite. Bill McClung, Appalachian Power Company's Roanoke man in charge of arrangements, was called upon to deal with the matter. Oddly, there were no 100-watt bulbs immediately available, but, McClung has said dryly, "it didn't take long for the housekeeping people to find them." AEP's managers were meeting again at the Hotel when the Northeast blackout of 1967 struck. AEP's utility systems experts were called away immediately from the Roanoke meeting by the Federal Power Commission to help investigate the cause of the widespread calamity, and so created a number of vacant rooms in the Hotel.

Celebrities of the Sporn-Romulo-MacDonald stripe aside, it was politics and politicians who were ever drawn to the Hotel along with all their works and pomps and impedimenta. "Alex" Alexander always liked to see the hue-and-cry of political conventions, the rallies, breakfasts, and receptions, in the Hotel, for, though they always posed clean-up problems, "the sticks from all the placards and signs made great tomato stakes."

John Eure, indefatigable reporter and pungent observer, met many of the movers, shakers and headliners over the years. One was Alben Barkley, then a senator from Kentucky. Eure took a photographer with him on his interview assignment, but it turned out that there was to be no photo opportunity. Barkley, in his underwear, met Eure at the door to his suite. "He was an amiable Southern gentleman," Eure recalls. "He told jokes, he offered me a drink, and I had a terrible time getting away."

One Sunday afternoon on the Hotel's porch, Eure, as a green reporter, met James Price, a Virginia politician of some stature and nerve—and as things turned out, prudence. Even though he was not part of the political so-called "machine," he had nevertheless built up substantial support and was running for governor, though it was not his ordained turn. To one question, Eure not only didn't get an answer, but in fact had to promise not to quote Price as even declining to answer. The result: no story. "I was wholly taken in by this charming politician," Eure confessed.

Senator John Warner, referring to the Hotel as a gathering place for the politicos, has written that "the rocking chairs on the front porch rocked some political careers and made others. I remember many a night falling asleep to the wonderful sounds of passing coal trains." He added that "Hotel

Chef Heinz Schlagel, preparing for Thanksgiving 1980, removes a well-done turkey from the oven

Roanoke had the best food and service—it was gracious, traditional Southern hospitality."

Susan Aheron Magell, Warner's chief of staff at the time and a native Roanoker, remembers playing a recital in the Hotel as a first grade piano student of Mrs. Edgar Foley, and being awed by the sight of an older student in a "beautiful, floor-length Scarlett O'Hara dress...I vowed to return when my knees stopped knocking." And she did, for political events involving all three of the political figures for whom

she worked—Caldwell Butler, John Dalton and John Warner. (And for her wedding day.)

James Olin remembers the night his wife Phyllis came to Roanoke for the first time. He had been recently transferred to Roanoke by General Electric Company. "We were settled down for a good night's sleep on the third floor, when all hell broke loose in the hall and in the rooms on both sides of us. It turned out that the annual convention of the Beta Club sorority was in the Hotel. Those teenagers kept going until three in the morning." Later speaking of his long career as a Representative, Olin recalled "the many command performances I attended to explain my voting in Congress." He remembered too a "Symphony Ball attended by John Warner, then a candidate for the Senate, and his new wife, Elizabeth Taylor."

For Senator Charles Robb, "the Hotel will alway be central to my earlier recollections of the Roanoke Valley...I couldn't count the number of times I stayed there—and even the greater number of times I visited all kinds of conventions, meetings, breakfasts, lunches, dinners...I particularly enjoyed the Hotel's peanut soup and its Sunday brunch." Robb's most memorable visit to the Hotel was in January 1982, when the Roanoke Valley Chamber of Commerce brought 80 members of the Virginia General Assembly via special train to Roanoke for a show-and-beg visit. Scheduled in addition to tours and presentations, there was to be "more than a little partying," and a black-tie dinner dance in the Ballroom.

Robert Garland, a veteran political activist, recalls the reception arranged at the Hotel in 1963 by Nelson Rockefeller during his run for the Republican nomination for president.

Garland stood in the reception line with Mrs. Rockefeller, and the line of guests reached from the Shenandoah Room down Peacock Alley, through the lobby and out into the parking lot. At the end of the reception Mrs. Rockefeller, thanking "Shorty" Leftwich for his services as headwaiter, gave him the floral display from the reception's main table.

Counting Rockefeller there have been five vice presidents of the United States to have stayed in Hotel Roanoke: Spiro Agnew, George Bush, Gerald Ford and Richard Nixon, and three of them became president. Add Ronald Reagan, who visited on political matters when he was governor of California, and Jimmy Carter, who campaigned there for himself.

Agnew's visit as a candidate for vice president on the Republican ticket with Nixon is recalled by Ray Garland, former Virginia state senator and a Republican party activist. Garland was in charge of the arrangements. "Since Maryland had no lieutenant governor, Agnew still functioned as head of state, and we were told he had to have a direct phone line to Annapolis installed in his suite. That was quite a job and we had to pay for it—several hundred dollars, I think.

"Agnew's family was with him and we were told his daughters liked to send out for late pizza and we should have a menu available…If they had any Roanoke pizza it is a fact lost to history." Fred Walker says that Agnew— "gracious and charming"— invited him to sit down and chatted about earlier visits to Roanoke, where he said his grandmother had lived.

Another telephone, this one red, played a major role in the visit to the Hotel by Vice President Nelson Rockefeller.

Ronald Reagan, when he was governor of California, spoke at the Hotel on behalf of Republican candidates

Janet Jenkins, the manager, had always said that running a hotel was the ideal job for a woman, because it was nothing but running a household, except on a larger scale (this in a period with a less intensive view of gender roles), and "where every guest was treated as a special person." For the visit of the Vice President of the United States, a special person by any measure, she played the ultimate hostess and gave up to him her own apartment in the Hotel—living room, two bedrooms, two baths, entry, kitchen, butler's pantry—as the only appropriate space available. Coming in to the Hotel, the vice president was kept by the Secret Service in a "holding room" until all security arrangements were checked; Mrs. Jenkins remembers being not happy with the idea of the Secret Service going through her dresser drawers looking for bombs. The Secret Service also installed a red phone to keep Rockefeller in touch with the White House. The next morning, after Rockefeller had left, the phone briefly was still there, though disconnected, and "I touched it before they came to get it," Janet Jenkins admits. He took room service meals, the principal feature of which was a steak prepared by Chef Heinz Schlagel.

Vice President Gerald Ford was a visitor in July 1974, brought to Roanoke on a political mission of some sort. He was put up in the so-called "Presidential Suite," a collection of rooms on the third floor. The designation referred not to the Washington presidents, but to the Roanoke ones, those working across the street in the railroad's General Offices. Its use was not exclusive to those presidents—it was rentable by anyone who fancied the space and was willing to pay the premium price. The suite was furnished, according to Janet Jenkins, not in the cool, airy, colorful style of the rest of the guest rooms, but in the over-wrought fashion of the late Victorian era, when the Hotel was built. "A lot of fringes and heavy curtains and dark colors and perhaps plush; there was a round settee in the middle of the living room. A man told me he thought it looked like a brothel. I told him I didn't know, but that I would take his word for it."

She recalled Ford as a nice man who "emanated a wonderful warmth and disposition, but just the same the visit was a trying thing—a heavy responsibility."

Warren Webb tended to the needs of Alabama Governor George Wallace during a Hotel Roanoke stop in his campaign for the presidential nomination. One of those needs was a large steak dinner he delivered to the Governor's room, along with a large fruit basket. The entire thing had to be undone to permit the Secret Service to examine it

piece by piece. There was also a stethoscope somehow involved in the examination. One Secret Service agent told Webb that the Hotel was "the nicest place we've been in."

Vice President George Bush ate his dinner at a table in the middle of the Regency Room's dance floor with his Secret Service detail at nearby tables, and earlier, roaming around the Hotel lobby had encountered General Manager Peter Kipp. "Hiya, Peter, how ya doin?"

Private citizen Richard Nixon was in the Hotel in 1966 speaking on Vietnam, and President Richard Nixon was in the Hotel the night before Linwood Holton's election as governor. Walker conducted Nixon to his suite on the latter occasion. For his dinner he ordered only bouillon and dry toast, but insisted that his Secret Service detail get whatever they wanted. "An interesting man," is Walker's judgment. The Republican party twice nominated Holton for gover-

Vice President Gerald Ford is greeted in the Hotel lobby by Janet Jenkins, general manager, and Norfolk and Western Railway's John R. Turbyfill, later Norfolk Southern's vice chairman

Hotel business was not all political carryings-on and conventions and dinners. There were extravagant flower shows as well. The top picture, taken in May 1933, shows a setting for tea with floral display. In the other photograph (unknown date) the Ballroom was the scene either of another flower show or a major social event

nor in uproarious celebrations, with Ronald Reagan speaking at the 1969 Convention, and in November of that year celebrated victory in the Crystal Ballroom. (A visitor to the Hotel on many occasions, he is remembered by Warren Webb as an outgoing friendly man who would often take his meals with the Chef and some of the staff at the Chef's table in the kitchen.) Presidential candidate Jimmy Carter spoke to his party's faithful in 1976. In 1988, Oliver North, facing hooting demonstrators, drove up to the Hotel with a police escort and went inside to speak at a Marshall Coleman campaign breakfast, and declared he would not forget how Coleman had stood up for him in his own troubles.

Even taking into account the eminent figures—political and

otherwise—who have foregathered at the Hotel, certainly the grandest convocation there—and possibly in the entire Commonwealth—occurred on Virginia Night in December 1967. Governor Mills Godwin and all six of his living predecessors—J. Lindsay Almond, John S. Battle, Colgate W. Darden, Albertis S. Harrison, Thomas B. Stanley and William M. Tuck—and their wives were guests of honor at a banquet and dance in the Crystal Ballroom. Not since the stars were painted on the ceiling of the Oval Room 30 years before had the Hotel seen such a constellation.

The idea of the gathering came from discussions between Carl Thurston, the suave, sophisticated promotion-minded man who succeeded George Denison as general manager in 1964, and Fred Walker, then sales manager and later general manager. (Walker is the only Hotel Roanoke general manager to have attended Oxford University. Stationed in England during the Second World War, he took advantage of a special Army program and spent nine months studying in Balliol College and living in the same rooms which in the last quarter of the 19th century housed Herbert Asquith, who became prime minister in 1908. Doreen Hamilton Fishwick's distinction is that she is only Hotel Roanoke general manager to have sung professionally on the operatic stage.)

Virginia Night's invitation list included the heads of the 100 top corporations in Virginia. With the railroad's logistical cooperation and fueled by the determination to make it a newsworthy as well as a memorable event, Walker traveled aboard a Norfolk and Western Railway office car to New York to fetch Charlotte Curtis, the gifted women's editor of *The New York Times*. It was the first time she had ever ridden on an office car. Joining the trip in Washington on

the return trip were Herb Blunk, former president of the American Hotel and Motel Association, and senior vice president of Hilton Hotels, and Richard Joseph, travel editor of *Esquire* magazine, who had flown to Washington from overseas. The luggage of this sophisticated world traveler, Walker remembers, was tied up with a piece of rope. The next morning, the tireless Walker in the NW aircraft ran a shuttle from Roanoke around the state to pick up most of the guests of honor.

Dinner started with seafood cocktail a la Russe, went on to tomato bouillon with cheese straws, poached filet of turbot with lobster wine sauce, roast tenderloin of beef, with stuffed mushrooms a la Virginienne, pesillees potatoes, fiddleheads, hearts of palm salad, cherries jubilee and coffee. There were two wines—Haut Sauternes 1964, and Chateau Lafitte 1961—and liqueurs.

And what are fiddleheads, Ms. Curtis wanted to know. Walker said that they are young fern sprouts, imported, and supposed to taste like beans. Lieutenant Governor Fred Pollard said that "they don't look like anything that grows around here." Ms. Curtis reported to readers of the *Times* that "Everybody seemed to like them."

The stars of the show, the governors, were "amiable, well-mannered and venerable," Curtis wrote. "They came from all over their beloved state to this their western frontier to drink, dine and dance at what was ostensibly the 85th anniversary of Hotel Roanoke...They were done up in dinner jackets of various eras, and during the ensuing cocktail reception, when they weren't being cornered by the other guests, they wrapped their arms around one another and talked about old times."

Not since the stars were painted on the ceiling of the Oval Room 30 years before had the Hotel seen such a constellation.

89

*A great night for
Virginians occurred in
December 1967, when
the Governor and six of
his predecessors were in
the Hotel to celebrate its
85th birthday. Seated,
Thomas B. Stanley,
the then Governor
Mills Godwin,
John S Battle;
standing,
William M. Tuck,
Colgate W. Darden,
Albertis S. Harrison,
J. Lindsay Almond*

She added that the Rev. Noel C. Taylor, president of the Roanoke Ministers' Conference and pastor of High Street Baptist Church (and later a many-term mayor of Roanoke), delivered the invocation and benediction. "He too represented an old Virginia family; his ancestors were among the first slaves."

In these political events, most of which she observed from her various job assignments, Janet Jenkins preserved a pretty neutrality: "I was a Republican, then I was a Democrat, then I was a Republican again."

(Only three years before, after the passage of the Civil Rights Act, Janet Jenkins had welcomed the first black guest into the Hotel. She was Mahalia Jackson, the distinguished gospel singer. Doing so was one of Mrs. Jenkins's proudest moments. The singer's agent had called from New York earlier to make the arrangements; on her departure Ms. Jackson stopped to thank Mrs. Jenkins for her "graciousness and courtesy." The incident "opened the door to a new and finer era in the Hotel's life," Mrs. Jenkins has said.)

Virginia Night with its spectacular menu pre-dated by several years the arrival in 1971 of Executive Chef Heinz Schlagel. Born in West Germany, he started his craft as a 15-year-old apprentice, and working in hotels all across Europe rose from assistant to the cook, cook, sous-chef and finally chef. Eventually he found his way to Montreal, where he met Ken Wilkey— "an outgoing personality"—and later to the Beverly Hillcrest Hotel in California. There he fed Hollywood luminaries—Dean Martin, William Holden and Anthony Quinn, among others. John Wayne liked a soup, a small serving of meat and a salad; Diahann Carroll liked a raw meat entree, though a fair observer would have reason to believe that the servings should be the other way around. When Wilkey was named general manager of Hotel Roanoke, he sent for his former colleague. Schlagel found the Hotel to be much like some hotels in Germany, "old style, comfortable-old."

He arrived on a Tuesday, and immediately had to prepare dinner for the Norfolk and Western Board of Directors Wednesday. It was a simple matter: consomme au riz, filet de sole marguerite, tournedos rossini, asparagus, a Belgian endive salad, cheese and fruit tray, petit fours with demitasses of Colombian coffee, followed by liqueurs. It lasted two hours. "I think it was a hit," he said later, buoyed by the compliments NW President John Fishwick and other directors extended. These Board dinners were highlights of Schlagel's Hotel career, when Fishwick selected the wines and took a hand in planning the menu.

Schlagel's cosmopolitan tastes and continental cusine brought what one observer has called a "significant improvement" to the Hotel's menu. He added more or less for the first time bouillabaisse, escargot and frog legs. But he also tried a "little bit of everything" in the kitchen and learned to like Smithfield ham and spoonbread. He never said "we can't do that," even when he was preparing something he had never prepared before—like coon and other game that was brought to him for special handling. He oversaw a crew of 20 to 30 people, including a baker, three breakfast cooks, and one person who fixed only sandwiches. Schlagel later went on to become chef at Roanoke's Shenandoah Club.

The Hotel in a 1947 snow scene

CHAPTER V

A Difficult Decision and What Followed From It

Early in the afternoon of July 26, 1989, Arnold B. McKinnon, Chairman of the Board and Chief Executive Officer of Norfolk Southern Corporation, sat in Hotel Roanoke's Pine Room, scene of many a revel in the Hotel's long and glittering history. With him, and about to make some history of their own—though without much revelry—were Dr. James McComas, president of Virginia Polytechnic Institute and State University, and Roanoke Mayor Noel C. Taylor and their assorted paladins. Then he stood up and told a room full of journalists and civic leaders that Norfolk Southern Corporation would donate its 107-year-old Hotel Roanoke to Virginia Polytechnic Institute and State University to be turned into a major facility for conferences and continuing education.

A few hundred words further into his statement McKinnon also announced that Norfolk Southern would build an office building in Roanoke to accommodate in a new and efficient environment its 1200 officers and office employees. Then spoke Dr. James McComas, the new president of Virginia Polytechnic Institute and State University.

"As a land grant institution, Virginia Tech has a unique mission to serve the needs of the people of Virginia. With this gift, Virginia Tech will establish a management/executive development and continuing education facility within the confines of a renovated and restored Hotel Roanoke. Virginia Tech," he said, "will lead the effort to restore the Hotel and return it to its rightful place as the grand dame of Roanoke's hotels...I thank Arnold McKinnon, John Fishwick and the board of Norfolk Southern Corporation for this important gift to the future of Virginia Tech and to the future of Roanoke."

In local newspaper coverage the next day, the gift of the Hotel took second place behind the office building announcement. Reaction to the latter by some of the city's mandarins, who had hoped the railroad would buy into plans for a new landmark office tower then under development, ranged from resignation through petulance to fury: "It would have been wonderful for the city," mourned one. "It's the railroad's way of telling Roanoke they're out of here; flowers on the grave," bleated another.

All of this, plus unseemly personal animus directed at Fishwick, is, even years after the event, hard to understand. After all, Norfolk Southern was preparing to make a $25-million-plus investment in Roanoke's downtown, a demonstration to even the slowest mind that the railroad and its works would remain and prosper in the city, as it had done for more than a century.

This is merely by-the-way. The major reason why the gift of the hotel didn't show up until the bottom of the second paragraph of the news story was simply that by then, it wasn't much of a surprise, as surprises go. Two weeks

...Fishwick told a reporter simply, "I know the Hotel is a problem in the long run; that's all I can say."

before the announcement, it was reported that Virginia Tech's Board of Visitors had authorized the administration to "submit a formal proposal to Norfolk Southern regarding the Hotel Roanoke." Roanoke city officials were quoted as being "extremely excited about the role Tech might play in plans for the conference center" and the conversion of Hotel Roanoke to a conference hotel, a project that in one form or another had been on the city's plate for a long time. And now it was approaching reality.

Playing his cards close, Fishwick told a reporter simply, "I know the Hotel is a problem in the long run; that's all I can say."

Then, on the day before McKinnon's press conference there

appeared a long and largely accurate story reporting what was about to occur. It was headlined "NS to give Tech hotel," and quoted Fishwick: "I think it's the greatest thing to hit Roanoke in my lifetime. We're going to change this town from a blue-collar town into a university town." Minnis Ridenour, executive vice president of Virginia Tech and its chief business officer, agreed: "We're betting on the long term impact of Virginia Tech and the impact it will have on Roanoke."

So, when McKinnon stood up to face the cameras and note-books most people knew what he was going to say about the Hotel. What they didn't know was what had brought Norfolk Southern to such a portentous step involving a hal-lowed Roanoke symbol.

A Hotel publicity photograph from the early 1960s sought to emphasize the Hotel as a family place to stay

As it happened, several events and conditions in Norfolk Southern and its hotel subsidiary became congruent in late 1980s. For one, Norfolk Southern's Annual Report for 1987 reported in austere prose (but not austere enough to exclude a pardonable note of pride) that Hotel Roanoke was "a real estate activity that contributed positive earnings....A restoration program begun in 1986, coupled with new marketing initiatives, returned the hotel operation to positive earnings for the first time in many years." Not a large sum, to be sure, but sufficient to allow the Hotel's proprietors to put away the red ink that had so lavishly and customarily ornamented the books since 1980. Further, "Capital expenditures of more than $1 million in 1987 and 1988 are being funded wholly from the hotel's internally generated cash flow." These expenditures involved principally remodeling and re-decorating its guest rooms, one floor at a time. (This work continued virtually up to the Hotel's closing. Later, asked about these expenditures at a time when no return on the investment was possible, McKinnon declared simply "as long as we had guests, we were determined to maintain quality.")

At the same time, such earnings as the Hotel was generating were clearly inadequate to finance the major—$32-35 million—capital expenditures needed mainly for a new heating and cooling system (principal source for some while of guest complaints), although there were other pressing requirements as well. Such a major program would be necessary to enhance quality and competitive standards, "to make it first class" in the words of Arnold McKinnon. Whatever happened, he added, "we recognized the need to handle the Hotel in a manner consistent with our citizenship in the Valley."

Was an investment of that magnitude by Norfolk Southern likely? Apparently not very. Norfolk Southern's future, McKinnon has said, suggested that the capital resources the Hotel would need might well be put to better use elsewhere. "Elsewhere" most certainly included a new General Office Building in Roanoke. The existing two office buildings, one built before the turn of the century, the other in 1931, were, like the Hotel across the street, old, increasingly inefficient, under-populated and costly to maintain. (The elevators in the older of the two were temperamental and given to whimsical and sometimes prolonged stops between floors. One employee said he tried to be sure whenever he entered the car that he had 1) been to the bathroom, 2) had with him something to read or eat, and preferably both.) McKinnon told the press conference that the "largest buildings were in need of repair and rehabilitation if we are to continue them in service...Our studies indicated that it would be more efficient and economic to consolidate the majority of our Roanoke personnel in a new building."

In October 1985 Fishwick, though he had retired as Norfolk and Western Railway's chairman and was at the time associated with a Washington law firm, had been prevailed upon by Norfolk Southern's then chairman, Robert B. Claytor, to return to Roanoke and oversee the Hotel's operations and to determine what, if anything might be done with it. He moved back into the penthouse where he and his family had lived for many years, just across the street from his railroad office. (A perhaps apocryphal story has it that during one of the country's perennial energy crises in the 1970s, a reporter asked Fishwick what he was doing to promote energy conservation. "I walk to work," he is supposed to have replied.)

From that aerie he watched over the property and absorbed its problems. His task was, he told a reporter at the time, a "sort of labor of love. I don't know if anything can be done." In truth the prospect he faced then was formidable: Hotel Roanoke had been losing money and would—except for 1987—continue this dismal course. The losses sometimes approached a million dollars a year. It was in debt to its owner and it faced major competition from local motels, which though lacking Hotel Roanoke's charm and tradition, nevertheless could offer its patrons state-of-the-art facilities beyond the Grand Old Lady's capabilities.

One thing he did was to hire a new general manager, Doreen Hamilton, a brisk, no-nonsense professional hotelier from Philadelphia's Barclay Hotel where she had been managing director. Her credentials included managerial experience at New York's American Stanhope and Barclay Hotels, and whose forte was cost-cutting and tight and accurate budgeting. She later said that she had to ask "Where is it?" when she was told about the job opening in Roanoke and she had not even heard of its eponymous Hotel. The work force she was to manage was still shaken from a six-month-long strike that had aroused deep and divisive feelings in the community, but she was quick to put those matters in the past, took charge and, as one former subordinate said, "got involved."

After a careful exploration of the books, she concluded that the Hotel could not be made financially stable in the presence of its large debts to the parent Norfolk Southern Corporation. With the understanding that the debt would be forgiven, she accepted the job. She had also discovered, as her former staff assistant Vickie Stump Cutting so succinctly put it, that "some Roanokers didn't pay their bills."

The books revealed significant outstanding debts run up and left unpaid for meals, parties, meetings and so on. Mrs. Hamilton had not been on the job very long when she began to pursue with considerable vigor the payment of these obligations. It was a situation, Mrs. Hamilton felt strongly, which could not be tolerated any further, and after a few hortatory telephone calls and a few clearly expressed letters, was gratified to see that indeed, it was not.

While all this was happening in the Norfolk Southern/Hotel Roanoke orbit, the city manager, looking at the possibility of a major conference/trade center to be associated with Hotel Roanoke, had formed a Trade Center Task Force in 1985 and undertaken a study by the public accounting firm of Laventhol & Horwath to determine the center's feasibility. This would be part of Roanoke's long-term development plan. The study's conclusion was yes, it was feasible, but only if a modern 300-400 room convention hotel was in support of it. Earlier Norfolk Southern and Dominion Bankshares (now First Union Bank), perhaps the entire region's principal banking institution, had collaborated on another study, this one by the RTKL firm, to look at the project from a different viewpoint: whether the Trade Center could support either a modernized Hotel Roanoke or a new convention-type hotel. The answer was affirmative. But "modern" was the operative word in both studies, which would seem to eliminate Hotel Roanoke as it then stood.

The person of David Caudill now assumes a major role in the labyrinthine events that ultimately led to the July 26 announcement. He was vice chairman of Dominion Bankshares, an alumnus of Virginia Tech, and chairman of the city's Trade Center Task Force. Indefatigable in his search for ways to make a trade center—or Conference Center or Exhibit Hall; concepts for all three circulated freely as the participants worked toward a useful focus—a viable reality for Roanoke, Caudill held frequent conversations with City Manager Robert Herbert and the city's economic development director, Brian Wishneff.

The three met frequently in Caudill's office, a place to "talk 'what-ifs' as a sort of debating society," Herbert later said. In meeting after meeting, "we just let matters develop. The loss of the Hotel would mean a major loss of business to the city; we all knew we didn't want that. At the same time, studies showed a need to maximize revenues from the

Civic Center. An Exhibit Hall—or whatever it would be called—would need a base-load permanent tenant to provide perhaps 25 per cent occupancy to make it viable. We talked of establishing a mart of some sort, a continuing event in the city—a medical mart, a rug mart, even. From there, it was a quick step in our 'what-if' sessions from rugs to an 'education mart,' and that meant Virginia Tech."

But what interest would Virginia Tech have in acquiring a hotel at all, much less one in Roanoke? Caudill knew how to find out.

It was about this time that Virginia Tech had found a new

Typical lobby scene, probably in the late 1940s

97

The press conference in July when Norfolk Southern announced the donation of the Hotel to Virginia Tech. Roanoke Mayor Noel C. Taylor speaks, flanked by Norfolk Southern's Arnold B. McKinnon, and Virginia Tech's Dr. James McComas

president, Dr. James McComas, president of the University of Toledo. He had not yet left the one for the other. Warner Dalhouse, Caudill's chief at Dominion, was eager to add McComas to his Board of Directors. He thought he and Caudill ought to take the bank's aircraft to Toledo and make the offer, and Caudill, Herbert and Wishneff saw the trip as a chance to explore the new president's interest in the Hotel/Conference Center issue. Four people went on the bank's aircraft to Toledo: the two bankers, Roanoke Mayor Rev. Noel C. Taylor and Herbert. Dr. McComas was about to have earnest visitors.

Herbert, in his approach, reminded McComas of Virginia Tech's mission as a land grant university—the Commonwealth as a campus, continuing education and outreach. McComas had no need of the sales pitch. His own University of Toledo had earlier become involved in a similar role with the city and an existing hotel. He was able to show the Roanokers a large computer-filled classroom where the University was conducting re-training education for employees displaced by an industrial shutdown, the idea at work. The visitors lunched with the McComases at their home. Not just the lunch but the visit was in Herbert's words "a love feast."

Thus, when McComas soon took up his station in Blacksburg, the University was prepared to move ahead. Tech's plenipotentiary was Minnis Ridenour, executive vice president and chief business officer, who soon joined the Herbert-Caudill discussion group. Ridenour, expanding on the "education mart" concept, began seeing the Hotel/Conference Center as an industry, an entity with profit and growth in mind, a position in no way incompatible with the Tech view of outreach and continuing education. The con-

ventional wisdom held that the Hotel couldn't stand alone, but with a Conference Center...?

Thinking on more or less parallel lines, was Norfolk Southern's man-in-the-hotel, Fishwick. Though primarily representing Norfolk Southern's interest, he shared with the others a desire to find a way to bring to reality a major meeting facility, settle the Hotel dilemma, and at the same time promote Tech's own goals.

Into this came the tireless Caudill, shuttling back and forth among the city, Virginia Tech and Norfolk Southern, like a Blue Ridge Metternich, carrying from one to the other sometimes oblique, sometimes vague ideas, scenarios, positions.

Finally, Fishwick, on his own and in his words, "without any backing or authorization from Norfolk [corporate headquarters] flat out" asked Caudill if Virginia Tech would consider accepting the Hotel as a gift. The question was welcome, because Tech had already come to the conclusion that it would. For Norfolk Southern, McKinnon approved this direct approach, seeing it, as he later told an interviewer, as a way "to demonstrate our commitment to the city of Roanoke by keeping Hotel Roanoke as a functioning entity, and to open a new level of cooperation with Tech and its continuing education and outreach programs." (Norfolk Southern's Board of Directors by action at its July 25, 1989, meeting made the donation of the Hotel to Virginia Tech official.) The city for its part agreed to supply an amount which eventually rose to $12.8 million for the Conference Center, which not only guaranteed a revived and operating Hotel Roanoke, but also fulfilled its own original dream.

...Caudill, shuttling back and forth among the city, Virginia Tech and Norfolk Southern like a Blue Ridge Metternich...

There was an all-star cast of players in this bravura performance, and it is one of the more rewarding reflections on the whole business that each of the principals was eager to extend large chunks of credit for its success to others. Fishwick said that "McComas had the courage and vision to see all of the disparate elements in this project, and grasp instinctively how it would benefit the community, the Hotel, and mostly his notion of what he wanted his University to be in the future." Ridenour and Herbert credit Caudill; Caudill credits Fishwick and Herbert. In turn, Herbert had special praise for the late Horace Fralin, who, though suffering from his terminal illness, devoted time and expended irreplaceable energy to work on the project. Virginia Tech, said McKinnon, played a "serendipitous role, providing continuity and commitment to Roanoke and a unique opportunity to the school."

So all of the converging tides, the disparate personalities and their egos, the elation, sorrow and promise met in the Pine Room on that summer day to mark a sad end and a brave beginning for Hotel Roanoke. For its employees, however, there was only the sad end.

Hamilton had earlier that day informed her senior managers of the forthcoming decision and they in turn informed their own staffs, supplemented by memos posted in employee work areas.

"We were shocked" at the melancholy news, according to Vickie Stump Cutting, administrative assistant to the general manager. "We didn't know what to say. A lot of us had thought that something had to happen—perhaps a chain taking over." Hotel employees like everyone else in the Roanoke Valley had read press reports about the donation of the Hotel to Virginia Tech, and earlier rumors about its sale. "Alex" Alexander and Billy Davis, however, were not especially shocked at the news; "we had heard the rumors— who hadn't?—and besides," said Billy later, smiling, "we were in a position to hear things."

Donation of the Hotel was one thing; but shutting it down was quite another, especially to employees, some of whom represented the third, even fourth generation of their families who had worked there, raised and educated their children and been a proud and living part of the Roanoke tradition. Not even the trauma of a six-month-long strike and the sometimes painful divisions and hard feelings which followed its settlement could dislocate the comradeship nurtured by the bad news.

"We were all in the same predicament," said Bruce Coffey, front desk manager at the time, in a later interview. "We consoled one another, encouraged one another. And above all, we kept the Hotel operating at its usual high standards. Whatever happened, we weren't going to change that. We still had our pride." (Years after the closing, many employees still kept in touch with each other. Billy Davis, "Alex" Alexander and Mike Mason lunch together regularly to relive their life-careers; Vickie Cutting, Bruce Coffey, Lynne Schumacher, former controller, and Mark Lambert, former engineer, in their own gatherings among other things talked Schumacher through her CPA study and listened to Lambert's reports on the renovation work on the Hotel where he worked for the contractor after the closing.)

CHAPTER VI

Setting Out The Deck Chairs

In this climate—made up in equal parts of determination, sorrow, uncertainty and pride—Doreen Hamilton, now Mrs. John P. Fishwick, had to continue to operate the Hotel and simultaneously prepare to shut it down November 30. There were arrangements to be made to dispose of the furnishings, cancel reservations and meetings scheduled after the closing date. Ranking in equal importance with all of these and other pressing matters was the question of any financial settlement with employees.

Although under the existing contract with Local 32 of the Hotel and Restaurant Union the Hotel was not required to make any severance payments to its unionized employees, Mrs. Fishwick took it as a matter of right that there should be a settlement "fair and honorable," in her words, and she so informed the Hotel's corporate masters in Norfolk headquarters. Concern for the well-being of employees and recognition of their importance to the success and reputation of the Hotel had always been a guiding principle in her management style. Indeed, at one point in her general managership she had wanted to provide a raise to all of the Hotel's employees, even though the union had not made such a request. Legally however this was impossible, for the curious reason that without union negotiations, the action would have been considered an unfair labor practice.

Calling local reporters to a press conference August 31, the general manager told them "We have some good news to share with you...As you are well aware both management and the employees have considered ourselves to be a family and I am delighted to report to you today that through the efforts of the Hotel and the union headed by Mr Minor Christian, we have reached a severance agreement which, as far as we know, is better than any severance offered hotel employees in the United States...

"Ever since...the announcement was made regarding the Hotel's closing, the Hotel's desire has been to lessen the burden which this closing may place on employees. We feel that this agreement will now allow the employees to take the time necessary to seek other employment or, in some cases, even to change their career paths.

"I have...assurances that our employees intend to see that the service offered at the Hotel Roanoke will continue to be of the highest quality right up until the last dinner is served and the last drink order is taken on the night of November 30."

Then, ever the consummate marketer, she added, "I trust that everyone will take the opportunity to visit this grand old lady at least one more time to sample the ambiance and the service which have been the very backbone of the Hotel Roanoke for the past 107 years and before she receives her new look for the 21st Century."

The agreement's terms were simple. Every person employed at the Hotel before July 26, 1989 (the day the closing was announced) would receive a week's pay at the employee's current wage rate for each year of employment. For full-

"...I trust that everyone will take the opportunity to visit this grand old lady at least one more time to sample the ambiance..."

time employees, the severance was based on a 40-hour week, for part-time employees on a 24-hour week. Minimum payments of $500 and $300 respectively were established. Those laid off because of lack of work would be eligible as well. Further, all employees would receive a letter of reference specifying that employment was terminated because of the Hotel's closing.

That matter settled, Mrs. Fishwick moved on to another. She had determined that the Hotel's passage from the railroad's ownership would best be marked with a spectacular, invitation-only Closing Banquet in the chandeliered Crystal Ballroom. She envisioned it as an event so dignified and steeped in traditional Hotel Roanoke graciousness that the

community would say of the Hotel with mournful pride, as Malcolm said of Cawdor, that nothing in its life became it like the leaving it.

The Closing Banquet was held November 28, 1989, and attendance was limited by space to about 600 invited persons, the standard seating capacity for a dinner to be followed by dancing. The event became what is known as a "hot ticket," prized by those who had one, coveted by those who didn't; Bruce Coffey fielded dozens of telephone calls from people who wanted to buy tickets. Because the dinner dance was essentially a local celebration of a local institution by local people, its guest list showed the Roanoke Valley's political and business magnificoes, movers and shakers, and a handful of Norfolk Southern's top echelon from Norfolk. Robert B. Claytor, Roanoke-born, former president of the Norfolk and Western Railway and at the time of the closing the retired chairman of Norfolk Southern, said it was "a bittersweet occasion." He recalled attending debutante balls in the Hotel in the late 1930s as a stag, "because I wasn't popular enough to be a date." Another Roanoker in the railroad party coming from Norfolk was John Turbyfill, then executive

On the Hotel's last day, Ray Ebbett, the lobby pianist, shares the keyboard with a small guest. Lights from the overhead chandelier are reflected on the piano's polished top

vice president-finance. He had a more agreeable recollection from his high school days: a rented tuxedo and the prettiest girl in school for a date. Also present at the Closing Banquet with his wife was Linwood Holton, former governor and a former Roanoker whose emotional connection to the city and Hotel operated at several levels. For the general public, 30 invitations were made available to those whose names were drawn at random from a fish bowl placed in the Regency Room.

Sitting down at tables for eight lining three sides of the Ballroom, women in fashionable-length dresses and men in black tie found at their places a handsomely designed and printed souvenir booklet. With the booklet and the arsenal of cutlery at each plate was a box containing a large brandy snifter emblazoned with the Hotel Roanoke seal, a gift which for many recipients would never be used, but put aside in a place of honor.

Titled "The Grand Old Lady on the Hill", the booklet's text, charting a course somewhere between soaring paean and melancholy epitaph, read:

> Hotel Roanoke opened Christmas Day, 1882, and closes the week after Thanksgiving, 1989, an embodiment of hospitality and service and elegance for more than a century. It was built in "pretty fields of wheat and corn" by the Norfolk and Western Railroad, one corner of a quadrilateral with a passenger station, a General Office Building and hammering, steamy railroad shops.
> Hotel Roanoke passes now to a new life. It is our hope—the management and the staff's—that this booklet will serve not only as reminder of this bit-

tersweet evening but to keep alive memories of honeymoons and dances, Fountain Room dates, political conventions, rehearsal dinners and wedding receptions, after-five aperitifs and a lazy sunning by the pool. Hotel Roanoke has been "our" Hotel to generations of Roanokers. In their name and on your behalf, we pause this evening and offer a toast to our Grand Old Lady on the Hill.

And thank you, Roanoke, for having been here.

The impeccable Hotel Roanoke service was, for this last gallant show, burnished to a even brighter perfection. As the Bruce Swartz Quintet played, a regiment of servers brought in dinner, anchored by the Hotel's traditional two culinary triumphs. The menu, printed in the booklet, consisted of peanut soup, sliced tenderloin of beef with fresh asparagus, glazed carrots and Duchess potato, spoonbread; and for dessert, twin mousse, raspberry puree, with tea or coffee. There were two Virginia wines.

After dinner, Doreen Fishwick proposed a toast to the Hotel's past, and its almost mystical union with the community that virtually grew under its gaze: "To her glorious past—may she sleep well, and may she awaken with all the charm of today to face a bright and prosperous 21st Century." And then, in a moment that brought tears to most, all sang a chorus of "Auld Lang Syne" It was at this moment, one man said, that the finality of what was happening came to him. "Up to then," he said, "it had been an abstract possibility, almost theoretical. Now, we all knew that we would never dance under these chandeliers again. It was sad." To join the singing, Mrs. Fishwick invited all of the dining service staff into the Ballroom to the cheers and

Patricia Banks delivers one last room service order before the Hotel closed

Dancing for the last time in the Regency Room

applause of the diners. In an emotional scene, guests and serving personnel hugged one another with sobs and tears. For Robert Garland, "it was probably the most elegant banquet ever held in the Crystal Ballroom...a truly memorable and magnificent occasion."

The dancing that followed until 11 o'clock was for many a poignant exercise and for one conjured up a comparison with a grimmer event: "it was like setting out deck chairs on the *Titanic*," he said.

If the Hotel was metaphorically setting out deck chairs, they were not being placed for passengers' comfort, but for sale. Agents of the National Content Liquidators, hired by the Hotel to dispose by sale of its entire contents had been working for nearly a week appraising and tagging the contents for sale, from coffee spoons to laundry equipment, beds to bath towels, televisions to teacups. The sale was to begin at 9 o'clock on Monday morning, December 4, three days after the close. Even on the Hotel's last day, NCL people were careful not to intrude on the sadness of the occasion as they prepared for the huge task awaiting them.

The last night for guests to stay in the Hotel was November 29, and about 100 of the rooms were taken. Those guests and scores of Roanokers spent part of November 30, prowling the still halls, lobby-sitting, strolling across the graceful Oval Room—always one of the city's loveliest public spaces—and reliving memories in the Crystal Ballroom. Staff continued their work briskly, attending to checkouts, serving lunch and other chores associated with both routine and closing. Charlotte Facella, sales director, had finished the painful task of notifying future conventions—some four or five years away—that their bookings could not be honored.

The big front door had its first and only lock installed. The Regency Room had no reservations left for the last night's dinner serving, and its intimate private space, the Virginia Room, was reserved by Robert Garland for a dinner with family and friends. (Gripped like several others by the recurring motif of the time and its mood of elegant fate, Garland noted that "like the band on the sinking *Titanic*, the music was still playing as we departed the dining room on that last night.") As the late autumn afternoon cooled and darkened, outside preparations moved ahead for the final flag-lowering, Taps-sounding, tear-shedding closing ceremonies around the Reflecting Pool.

Facing the three flagpoles and scores of old friends of the Hotel—at least two from as far away as California—flanked by the Noel C. Taylor Community Choir, a color guard, a Congressman, a State Senator and a Mayor, and watched from windows of the Norfolk Southern offices across the street, Doreen Fishwick had one more sad speech to give.

Sketching the old Hotel's century of history and citing its many firsts, she added "But now, with only seven hours left, we have gathered to say thank you and farewell. Thank you to this community, for 107 years ago you welcomed this Hotel into the life and mainstream of the Valley...to the Norfolk and Western Railway for having had the foresight to build a piece of history...and to the Norfolk Southern Corporation for their generous gift which will make the foundation upon which will be built a major presence of Virginia Tech...and...which will brighten the future and change the character of the Roanoke Valley.

"To the staff I say thank you for a job well done. You rose to the challenge, difficult as it was, and have kept the Hotel great to the last. To the people of this community, I say thank you for your support over the years.

When she said, "there will never be another Hotel Roanoke quite like this one," a man standing nearby was heard to mutter in a soft, Virginia-bred voice, "No, ma'am." Ending, she declared, "we who have worked here thank this grand old lady for affording us the privilege of being a part of her 107 years of service."

Rev. Noel C. Taylor, the city's black mayor, the same Noel C. Taylor mentioned by Charlotte Curtis in her *New York Times* account of the Hotel's Virginia Night in 1967, delivered the sort of eloquent and moving remarks that always characterized his public speech. "The Hotel Roanoke," he said, "has become a symbol to us all. Our citizens cherish its beauty and hold dear the memories of good times. But as we close its doors, lower the flags and sing the final notes, we also open the door to the future of our city."

With appropriate ritual and the sounding of the ghostly, evocative, simple notes of "Taps," the national, state and city flags were lowered and received by Congressman James Olin, State Senator Granger MacFarlane and Mayor Taylor on behalf of the Roanoke Valley History Museum. In the gloom, the shivering crowd, Hotel employees on the porch outside the Regency Room, the choir, the Fishwicks and perhaps even the watchers at the railroad's office windows sang "Auld Lang Syne." There could not have been many dry eyes.

Among the employees was Mike Mason, the bell captain, standing where he had stood for so many years, at the front door waiting for guests. He had worked at the Hotel during school summer vacations and had joined the Hotel permanently in 1946. Like his colleagues he felt sadness at the closing, but he was philosophical, even stoic: "It's not the end of the world," he said.

What he had seen in the years immediately preceding the fateful 1989 was worlds apart from what he called "the heydays" of the 1940s, '50s and early '60s. "The hotel was a hustle and bustle," he told Rebecca Burcher, writing for Norfolk Southern's employee publication, *NS World*. "We had business each and every day. From 4 p.m., we had lines. People were coming back and forth. Salesmen would be coming in off the road, and we were very busy every night, up till about 7 or 8 o'clock...In the heydays, it was a family situation. Everybody worked together. Everybody would speak when they saw you, and everybody would joke with you. And then everybody would go and do their work and do it well. It was a family." But now it was time for the family to leave home, and Mike Mason, before he too departed, went to do his work and do it well.

Invited into the Hotel this one last time for warm cider and cookies by the soon-to-be former general manager, and passing through the doors Mike Mason opened for them with his accustomed flourishes and smile, the hundreds who had stood in sadness outside brightened now in the Lobby and Oval Room and exchanged reminiscences.

Then after awhile they all went home and the door was locked behind them.

CHAPTER VII

Taking Home A Piece of the Past

The final act opened with the appearance onstage of National Content Liquidators of Dayton Ohio. It was then a 99-year old business that had grown and prospered from selling off the contents of hotels and other such institutions. NCL's offices in Dayton over the years had been furnished with antiques the company had bought for its own account, from chandeliers to paneling, and its walls were covered with prints, art and other memorabilia. Its collection was soon to be enhanced with items from Hotel Roanoke. Frank Long, NCL vice president, characterized Hotel Roanoke as "a pretty neat building" and "one of the more interesting" of the company's 600 contracts (another of which was the famed Dunes Hotel in Las Vegas, an unlikely yoke-fellow for Roanoke's "modern version of an old English inn").

For the privilege of selling large chunks of Roanoke's history, NCL had paid the hotel an undisclosed amount for the goods it would liquidate. The rumored figure at the time was a quarter-of-a-million dollars, subsequently characterized by Long as "close to accurate." What NCL itself earned from the liquidation was and remained proprietary information. It was to be an "everything goes" sale, continuing as

long as there was anything left to sell, which in the event was 17 days. The sale was vast in scale—"tens of thousands of pieces"—and in area—all guest floors, kitchens, laundry, Regency Room, Oval Room, Pine Room and the rest. Before it took place, however, a few exclusions were arranged. The large portraits of George Washington and Robert E. Lee were given to the Roanoke Valley History Museum, railroad memorabilia from the Whistle Stop was reserved for Norfolk Southern, food in the kitchen was given to Roanoke's TAP anti-poverty organization and unopened liquor was, under a special arrangement, sold back to the Virginia Alcohol Beverage Control Board store. The handsome paneling in the Lobby, chandeliers in the public rooms and ceiling fixtures in the guest rooms were declared exempt, reserved for the renascent Hotel Roanoke to come. Everything else was available and tagged and ready when the doors opened at 9 on the morning of December 4.

For days before the sale was to begin, NCL people had gone through the building, identifying, pricing and tagging everything, and taking care not to intrude on staff still occupied with running the Hotel. After November 30, when the last guest had departed and the door was locked, NCL assembled much of the sale merchandise in various places. For example, the Crystal Ballroom was stacked with silverware, china, glass and linens. Tables and chairs from the Regency Room were in the Shenandoah Room. Also in the Shenandoah Room more than 400 television sets were arranged, priced upward from $129. Guest room furnishings were kept in place. (During inventory, the NCL had discovered in a large upper floor closet an apparently forgotten cache of prints and a clock that was thought to have adorned the lobby. Long thought that "they had been up

...in the Shenandoah Room more than 400 television sets were arranged, priced upward from $129.

A buyer leaves the Hotel laden with some of its furnishings. Selling off the Hotel's entire contents took 17 days and drew thousands

there forty or fifty years." The prints went into the general sale; the clock went to Dayton where experts put its age at 200 years.)

NCL's press release in announcing the sale had noted that: "Private individuals can furnish their homes elegantly from our fine guest room suites. Hotel and apartment owners can furnish their units from our guest rooms." Also, "Business and private individuals will be interested in the large quantities of office furnishings and equipment," and "there are thousands of miscellaneous items such as the Steinway piano, all of the patio and pool side furniture, (and) all lobby furnishings." The NCL people on the job pointed out that unlike other hotels, which typically dispose of their furniture every five years or so, Hotel Roanoke traditionally refinished its chairs, tables, desks, and chests, some thought to be almost as old as the building itself. "They were good pieces to begin with, and they have the further advantage of age," which made them highly desirable, according to Long.

Although there were a significant number of commercial buyers on the extensive premises, by far the large majority of those who flocked through the Hotel for the sale were Roanoke Valley individuals who simply wanted something with a demonstrable Hotel Roanoke provenance for themselves, friends or family, or institutions, items for use as a continuing tie to the old place.

When the Hotel's door was re-opened at 9 on the Monday morning following the closing, December 4, there was already waiting in the cold winter wind a line of people stretching all the way around the building. Standing at the head of the line since 6:15 and by now uncomfortably cold

were Betty Carr Muse and Anne Hammersley, joined shortly by Mona Black, George Cartledge, Sr. and Charles Lunsford, representing Center in the Square, home to several of Roanoke's major cultural institutions. Enduring a couple hours' worth of cold, they were there to buy table settings for 72 to use for Center's receptions, luncheons or dinners in the area known as the Cartledge Connection, named for a major financial supporter and patron of the Center, who at that moment stood and shivered like everyone else in the long line.

The party had planned the buying spree carefully, having assigned specific duties to each so that no time would be wasted when they stepped into the sale's whirlwind to gather up the pieces. In the Crystal Ballroom, where sales, in Long's words, "went like firecrackers," they found, oddly, only 48 cups and saucers, and no water goblets at all with the HR logo, a shortage possibly explained by imputing pilferage to the Hotel's guests in the closing weeks. The Center's new dinner plates, salad plates, bread and butter plates ($7 to $9 each), what cups and saucers ($5 each) were available, and assorted knives, forks and spoons were put in ever-growing stacks in one corner of the Ballroom.

Protecting the heap from inquisitive eyes and grasping hands, Mona Black and Anne Hammersley covered it with their coats. Stationed there, Lunsford "stood like a sentinel" to fend off the ravening hordes roaming the Hotel. Cartledge had earlier arranged for cartons to be brought from his furniture establishment and into these went the table settings, wrapped in tablecloths and napkins, bought from stock as well. The boxes, a coffee urn, and nine round tables from the Regency Room and eight matching chairs for each were delivered by his trucks to the Center.

With "people running around and grabbing, the whole business was a combat mission" for Mona Black; and, in fact, in the course of picking out and holding on to these last pieces, a hand-to-hand combat indeed nearly did develop. Another buyer had decided that he would take two tables from those she had with some difficulty collected herself. "No," she declared firmly after a brief confrontation with the usurper. "That is unacceptable. These are my tables. Look for your own somewhere else."

The Hotel's events board, still showing the name of Ray Ebbett, the Lobby pianist, was marked $165, and bought for the Roanoke Valley History Museum by its director, Dr. Nancy Connelly. The Lobby bar went for $1,925 to a local Roanoke couple for their home. The planters that divided the bar from the Lobby proper were bought by a Roanoke restaurant, which also acquired additional Hotel Roanoke

flavor with the large table from the Oval Room, a number of mirrors and chairs from guest rooms and several pieces of kitchen equipment. An Atlanta firm bought the heavy-duty laundry equipment. The portrait of Kylene Barker, Miss Virginia/America, which had hung on the wall at the head of Peacock Alley, was priced—and bought—for $225. Long himself bought two dozen brandy glasses, and a partner at NCL bought the Steinway for his home.

Buyers lined up every one of the 17 days "as if they were waiting for a seat on a roller coaster," said Long. Inside at any one time, there were typically 1500 and 2000 potential buyers, and people were admitted in groups of 25 or so to replace those departing. Cashiers were set up in the major areas to take cash and credit cards, but no checks.

The Center in the Square people got everything they wanted. Their excursion, though sometimes fraught, was successful, as were uncountable others who came out of the Hotel laden with chairs, desks, framed prints, venetian blinds, champagne holders, waste baskets and other impedimenta. It was a clearly a success for NCL and ultimately in some ways for Hotel Roanoke itself. A success and satisfaction for many, but not everyone saw the sale in those congenial terms.

Bruce Coffey, front desk manager, in a starkly bare office. It was the last day of business

Robert Garland, who observed the life and times of the Hotel and its people with an almost Pepysian eye, was among those who went into the Hotel for the sale. Perhaps he witnessed the same sort of "running and grabbing" Black observed. The whole event resembled for him "a band of gypsies swarming down on their prey like killer bees. I could not watch as they disassembled and undressed her. I left empty-handed save for the memories. As I walked back to my car, I thought to myself that the Hotel had become a victim of the changing times. It had succumbed to the chrome and plastic crowd and the bottom line impresarios with their computers and their Teflon kitchens." Michael Ramsey was similarly affected. With a background in Roanoke's Chamber of Commerce and the Convention Bureau, he had nurtured a close and affectionate connection with the Hotel and its staff, and thought it was "a rather tawdry garage sale leaving nothing to symbolically tie the new hotel with the one it will replace."

A few days before Christmas, the sale came to end. Mrs. Fishwick and a small staff moved across the street to office space in the Norfolk and Western's executive suite to deal with final financial matters. In the Hotel, the lights were turned off, except for the few needed for security; the heat was turned off, except for what was needed to prevent mold and damp; the staff departed, except for the few needed to patrol the empty corridors. Everything that had given life and warmth and flavor and style to the life of Hotel Roanoke was gone, and it was left alone, silent and dark.

Silent, yes, and dark. But was it dead?

No, it was not. For like King Arthur, Hotel Roanoke fell asleep in its own Avalon, waiting for its time to come again. And come again it did, old memories preserved undimmed and brought to light once more.

> *For like King Arthur, Hotel Roanoke fell asleep in its own Avalon, waiting for its time to come again.*

HOTEL REVIVUS

At a rally in Roanoke's Civic Center on January 11, 1993, an event timed to allow live coverage for the six o'clock news by three television stations, Thomas Robertson announced that Renew Roanoke had raised $5 million for Hotel Roanoke and thereby assured its re-opening. (Not long after, Norfolk Southern contributed another $2 million, an amount 30 times what the railroad paid for the original Hotel.) It was the final and long-awaited piece in the financial package.

Robertson, Rev. Noel C. Taylor and David Bowers, Taylor's successor as mayor, had chaired the Renew Roanoke campaign. It lasted only seven weeks, involved 300 volunteers and three thousand contributors from all over the country, but mostly from the Roanoke Valley, all moved by fond memories of the place.

Renew Roanoke was born in a sense of urgency. Virginia Tech had set a deadline of December 31, 1992, for the financing of the re-opening of the Hotel. By late fall there remained a major dollar gap. The entire community took up the challenge and in an unprecedented fund-raiser over the Christmas holidays succeeded. Its success was more than sentiment–it was also, as Robertson said later, sound economics; for its millions, Roanoke not only preserved and enhanced Hotel Roanoke, but also became a one-third owner with the Virginia Tech Foundation.

The way was clear. Hotel Roanoke would live.

Renovation of the Hotel began with interior demolition

Rendering of the renovated Hotel Roanoke and the new Conference Center

POSTSCRIPT

The Renew Roanoke effort, splendid in spirit and result though it was, represented only a part of what was needed if Hotel Roanoke was to survive and prosper.

The Virginia Tech Foundation, Inc. discovered shortly that financing a hotel during the economic downturn of the early 1990s was difficult. The distress and closings of many hotels nationwide suggested that a conventional loan for the renovation of Hotel Roanoke was unlikely.

With this in mind, the Virginia Tech Foundation recruited a group of Roanoke Valley civic and business leaders to assist in constructing a financing and development package for the project. Members of the ad hoc group were well-known. They included the late Horace Fralin, president of the Foundation and of his own company, Fralin and Waldron, Inc.; Tom Robertson, president, Carilion Health System and co-chair of Renew Roanoke; David Caudill, vice chairman, First Union (Dominion) Bank; John Rocovich, Moss and Rocovich, P.C.; George Cartledge, Jr., president, Grand Piano and Furniture Co.; James Harvey, member, Roanoke City Council; Joseph Stephenson, president, Shenandoah Life Insurance Co.; Bob Herbert, Roanoke city manager; and Minnis Ridenour, executive vice president and Dr. Raymond Smoot, vice president for finance and treasurer, both of Virginia Tech.

In the face of difficulties and the demands of individual job responsibilities, this public-spirited group, working with six financing institutions, the U.S. Department of Housing and Urban Development, the City of Roanoke, the Virginia Tech Foundation and the Hotel Roanoke's new operating company, Doubletree Hotels Corporation, and including the Renew Roanoke campaign, produced a $27.5 million package. This guaranteed that Hotel Roanoke would not only survive, but thrive.

The story of financing, construction and re-opening of the Hotel has its share of disappointment, perseverance and triumph, and deserves to be told at a future time.

HOTEL ROANOKE

1882
October. George L. Jacoby, Hotel manager, registers first guests; December 25, Hotel officially opens

1890
Addition creates sun parlor, raises room total to 94

1898
July. Major fire closes hotel

1916
New three-story, 72-room wing added

1931
New four story and garage added at a cost of $225,000

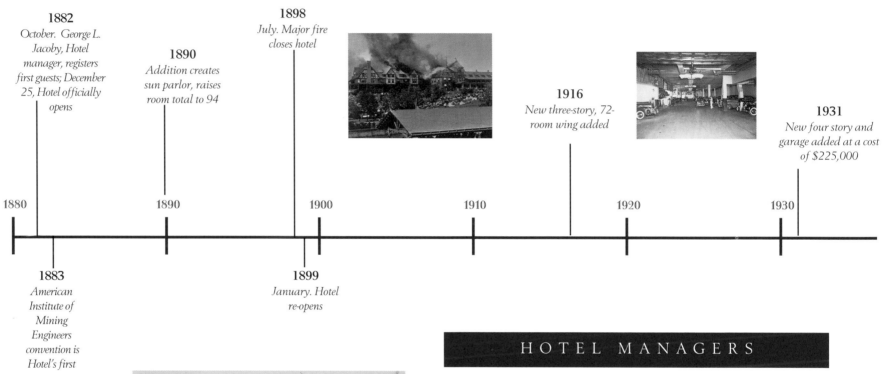

1880   1890   1900   1910   1920   1930

1883
American Institute of Mining Engineers convention is Hotel's first

1899
January. Hotel re-opens

HOTEL MANAGERS

George L. Jacoby, *1882-1888*
Fred Foster, *1888-1893*
S. K. Campbell, *1893-1901*
Fred Foster, *1901-1915*
Mrs. Fred Foster, *1915-1922*
W.A. Dameron, *1922-1928*
Fay M. Thomas, *1928-1930*
Kenneth Hyde, *1930-1935*
George Denison, *1935-1938*

Kenneth Hyde, George Denison, co-managers, *1938-1963*
George Denison, *1963-1964*
Carl Thurston, *1963-1969*
Fred Walker, *1969-1971*
Ken Wilkey, *1971-1976*
Janet Jenkins, *1976-1980*
Peter Kipp, *1980-1986*
Doreen Hamilton Fishwick, *1986-1989*

TIME LINE

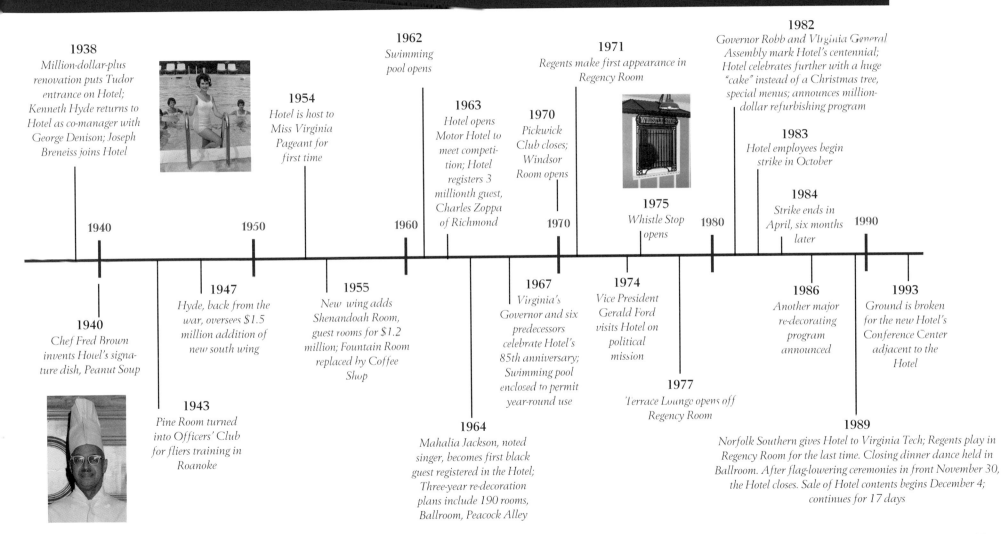

1938
Million-dollar-plus renovation puts Tudor entrance on Hotel; Kenneth Hyde returns to Hotel as co-manager with George Denison; Joseph Breneiss joins Hotel

1962
Swimming pool opens

1971
Regents make first appearance in Regency Room

1982
Governor Robb and Virginia General Assembly mark Hotel's centennial; Hotel celebrates further with a huge "cake" instead of a Christmas tree, special menus; announces million-dollar refurbishing program

1954
Hotel is host to Miss Virginia Pageant for first time

1963
Hotel opens Motor Hotel to meet competi-tion; Hotel registers 3 millionth guest, Charles Zoppa of Richmond

1970
Pickwick Club closes; Windsor Room opens

1983
Hotel employees begin strike in October

1975
Whistle Stop opens

1984
Strike ends in April, six months later

1940   **1950**   **1960**   **1970**   **1980**   **1990**

1947
Hyde, back from the war, oversees $1.5 million addition of new south wing

1955
New wing adds Shenandoah Room, guest rooms for $1.2 million; Fountain Room replaced by Coffee Shop

1967
Virginia's Governor and six predecessors celebrate Hotel's 85th anniversary; Swimming pool enclosed to permit year-round use

1974
Vice President Gerald Ford visits Hotel on political mission

1986
Another major re-decorating program announced

1993
Ground is broken for the new Hotel's Conference Center adjacent to the Hotel

1940
Chef Fred Brown invents Hotel's signa-ture dish, Peanut Soup

1943
Pine Room turned into Officers' Club for fliers training in Roanoke

1977
Terrace Lounge opens off Regency Room

1964
Mahalia Jackson, noted singer, becomes first black guest registered in the Hotel; Three-year re-decoration plans include 190 rooms, Ballroom, Peacock Alley

1989
Norfolk Southern gives Hotel to Virginia Tech; Regents play in Regency Room for the last time. Closing dinner dance held in Ballroom. After flag-lowering ceremonies in front November 30, the Hotel closes. Sale of Hotel contents begins December 4; continues for 17 days

How to Make Hotel Roanoke Peanut Soup

2 quarts chicken broth

1 pint peanut butter

1 small onion (diced)

1/2 cup ground peanuts

1/4 pound butter

1/3 teaspoon celery salt

2 branches celery (diced)

1 teaspoon salt

3 tablespoons flour

1 tablespoon lemon juice

Melt butter in cooking vessel and add onion and celery. Saute for five minutes (not brown). Add flour and mix well. Add hot chicken broth and cook for a half hour. Remove from stove, strain, and add peanut butter, celery salt, salt and lemon juice. Sprinkle ground peanuts on soup just before serving. Serves 10.

How to Make Hotel Roanoke Spoonbread

1-1/2 cups corn meal

5 eggs

1/8 pound butter

2 cups milk

1 teaspoon sugar

1-1/2 cups boiling water

1-1/3 teaspoon salt

1 teaspoon baking powder

Mix corn meal, salt and sugar together and scald with boiling water. Add melted butter. Beat eggs and add milk to eggs. Combine two mixtures and add baking powder. Pour into baking pan and bake 30-40 minutes at 350 degrees. Serves ten.

Following is a list of those who contributed to the Renew Roanoke campaign, which raised $7 million towards the reopening of Hotel Roanoke.

Corporations

Acme Business Machines
Acorn Construction, Ltd.
Advance Auto Parts
Affiliated Podiatrists & Foot Surgeons
Air Filter Systems, Inc.
Akzo Coatings, Inc.
Alexander's
Allied Sales Company
Allright Roanoke Parking, Inc.
Allstate Foundation
American Drum
American General Finance, Inc.
Anderson & Reed
Anonymous (several donors)
Appalachian Investment Company
Architectural Wood
The Atlantic Mutual Companies
Automatic Equipment Sales of Roanoke
Autumn Corporation
Avis Construction Company
Avis Rent A Car
B. Willson Porterfield, Jr. Foundation
The Balmoral, Inc.
The Bandroom, Inc.
Baptist Minister Conference
Becker Clinic of Chiropractic
BellSouth Communications Systems
Beltone Hearing Aid Center
Billy's Ritz
Bio Gro Systems, Inc.
Blue Ridge Beverage Company, Inc.
Blue Ridge Foods Inc/3 Lil Pigs BBQ
Blue Ridge Moulding & Frame, Inc.
Blue Ridge Regional Business Journal
BMS, Inc.
Books First, Ltd.
Boone & Company
Brambleton Family Physicians, PC
Brambleton Junior Woman's Club
The Branch Group, Inc.
Brides House & Formals
Bright Services
Brothers Bakery, Inc.
Brown, Edwards & Company
Business Communications Systems
C & P Telephone Company
Calla Lily, Ltd.
Campbell Construction & Development
    Company
Cardinal Cabinet Corporation
Caremark
Carilion Health System

Carter Machinery Company, Inc.
Carter, Brown & Osborne, PC
Cash Book
Catawba Capital Management, Inc.
Center for Employment Law
Center for Rehabilitation & Development,
    Inc.
Central Fidelity Bank Roanoke
Charcoal Steak House
Charles B. Farrelly & Associates, Ltd.
Charles P. & Marion G. Lunsford Charitable
    Trust
Chas. Lunsford Sons & Associates
Chesapeake X-Ray Corporation
Cirlan, Inc.
CocaCola Bottling Company of Roanoke
Coleman & Massey, PC
College of Health Sciences
Colonial Outdoor Advertising
Commonwealth Medical Supply
Commonwealth Transportation Board
CommuniCorp, Inc.
Construction Services of Roanoke, Inc.
Coopers & Lybrand
Corned Beef & Company, Inc.
Cox Cable Roanoke, Inc.
Craigie, Inc.
Crestar Financial Corporation
Crystal Clear, Inc.
Crystal Spring Deli
CTSH/Sarsfield
Cundiff Drug Store, Inc.
Custom Wood Products, Inc.
Cycle Systems, Inc.
D. C. Shanks Chapter 31 R.A.M.
Data Makers, Inc.
Data Systems Consulting, Inc.
David D. Graybeal & Associates
Davidsons
Davis H. Elliot Company, Inc.
Design Business Interiors, Inc.
Dillard Paper Company
Dixon, Hubard & Feinour, Inc.
Dominion Bankshares Corporation
Dominion Forms Service/Quikprint
Dragon Corporation
Drs. Blum, Newman, Blackstock &
    Associates
E. K. Williams & Company
Elbert H. & Evelyn J. Waldron Charitable
    Foundation
Eldercare
Emily W. Kelly Foundation, Inc.
Emtech Laboratories, Inc.
Entre Computer Center Olympus Systems

Environmental Protection Systems
Erie Insurance Group
Errand Express
Evergreen Development Company, Inc.
Ewald-Clark, Inc.
Executone Communications, Inc.
F & W Management Corporation
Fabricated Metals Industries, Inc.
Fallon Florist
Fast Service Laundry & Cleaning, Inc.
Ferguson Enterprises, Inc.
Ferguson-Andrews
FiberCom, Inc.
Fincastle Herald
Fink's Jewelers, Inc.
First Fridays at Five, Inc.
Foot Levelers, Inc.
Foster Medical Supply, Inc.
Foti, Flynn, Lowen & Company, CPA
The Foundation for Roanoke Valley
Frame 'N Things & The Gallery
Frank L. Moose Jeweler, Inc.
Fret Mill Music Company
Fuel Oil & Equipment Company, Inc.
Fulton Motor Company, Inc.
G. J. Hopkins, Inc.
G.M.H. Clinical Laboratory, Inc.
Gallery 3
General Electric Drive Systems
GHC, Inc.
Gibson Radiator Shop, Inc.
The Gift Niche
Giggle Grams & Happy Time Balloons
Gill Memorial Eye, Ear, Nose & Throat
    Clinic, PC
Giulio Corsini Tailoring
Glad Rags, Inc.
Graham-White Manufacturing Company
Grand Piano & Furniture Company
Graphics Etc. Galleries, Ltd
Greater Roanoke Valley Development
    Foundation
Green Up Lawns & Landscapes
Greenway Court Flowers
H. L. Lawson & Son, Inc.
Hall Associates, Inc.
Hamlar & Curtis Funeral Home, Inc.
Harris Office Furniture Company, Inc.
Harvey Properties
Hayes, Seay, Mattern & Mattern
Heironimus
Holland-Richards Vault Service
Honey Tree Child Care Center, Inc.
Drs. Houghton & Wheelock, Ltd.
HST Signs

Industrial Cleaning Service
Industrial Development Authority
J. Berna Sales Company
J. Hunter Miller, Contractor
J. M. Turner & Company, Inc.
J. P. Turner & Brothers, Inc.
J. Weiner & Company, Inc.
Jefferson Surgical Clinic, Inc.
John C. Nordt Company, Inc.
John Lambert Associates, Inc.
John M. Oakey Funeral Service
Johnson & Higgins of Virginia, Inc.
Jolly, Place, Fralin & Prillaman
Jones & Jones Associates
JPD Investments, Inc.
Junior League of Roanoke Valley VA Inc.
Junior Women's Club of Vinton
Kay's
Kemba Roanoke Federal Credit Union
Kessler Associates, Ltd.
King & Higgs, PC
Kings Entertainment
Knights of Pythias, Osceola - Roanoke,
    Lodge # 47
KPMG Peat Marwick
Lamar Advertising
Landis & Gyr Powers, Inc.
Landis Interiors & Service
Lanford Brothers Company, Inc.
Lawrence Perry & Associates, Inc.
Lawrence Transportation Systems
Lawyers Title Insurance Corporation
Lee Hartman & Sons, Inc.
Leggett Department Stores, Inc.
Leisure Publishing Company
Lemon & Lambdon, Inc.
Lewis-Gale Foundation
Lone Wolf Enterprises, Inc.
Longaberger Baskets of Virginia
Lucas & Boatwright
Lucas Construction Company
Lumsden Associates, PC
Lunsford Realty & Investment
M & M Brokerage Company, Inc.
M. A. Sikes Design Company
Magee, Foster, Goldstein & Sayers
Magic City Motor Corporation
Malcolm Blue Print & Supply
    Corporation
Malcolm's Roanoke Valley Map
Mamie Vest Associates
Marco Supply Company, Inc.
Mario Industries of Virginia, Inc.
Martin Brothers Contractors, Inc.
Martin Travel, Inc.

Martin's German Service
Marylou, Ltd., Realtor
Martin, Kirkland & Bolling, Inc.
McClung & Meador, PC
McDonough Caperton Insurance
McKenney Russell Advertising
McLeod & Company
McNeil Asphalt Maintenance, Inc.
Meadow Spring Land & Realty
Medeco Security Locks, Inc.
Milan Brothers
Mills, Oliver & Webb, Inc.
Moore's
Moss & Rocovich, PC
Mouldings Unlimited, Inc.
Mountain Top Orchards
Muncy & Muncy, Inc.
Musselwhite & Associates
National D-Day Memorial Foundation
National Pools of Roanoke, Inc.
NationsBank Corporation
Nelson Limited Partnership
Neuhoff Farms, Inc.
New Fitness
The New Southern, Inc.
New Yorker Delicatessen, Inc.
Newbern-Trane
Norfolk Southern Corporation
Northwest True Value Hardware Company
NSW Corporation
Nuts & Sweet Things
Obenchain's Greenhouses, Inc.
The Office Supply Center of Roanoke
Old Dominion Data Systems, Inc.
Omni Import Parts
Orvis Company, Inc.
Otis Elevator Company
PaineWebber, Inc.
Pargo's Restaurant Roanoke Valley
The Park Oak Grove
Parvin, Wilson, Barnett & Guynn
Petroleum Marketers, Inc.
Phoenix Earth Store, Inc.
Physicians to Children, Inc.
Piedmont Aviation Services
Pitman Construction Company, Inc.
Plant Culture, Inc.
Plastics One, Inc.
Premier Rehabilitation Services
Professional Therapies of Roanoke, Inc.
Progress Printing Company
Property Maintenance Corporation
PYA Monarch
Quality Clothes, Inc.
Quality Produce Company, Inc.

Radford Community Hospital
RapidSign
Record Depot/County Sales
Red Bird Garage, Inc.
Reed's Automotive, Inc.
Reid & Russell Florist
RevCar Fasteners, Inc.
Richardson & Kirmse, Inc.
Richardson-Wayland Electric
    Corporation
Roanoke & Botetourt Telephone
    Company
Roanoke Animal Hospital
Roanoke Chapter of Girl Friends, Inc.
Roanoke Chapter of the National
    Railway
Roanoke Construction Specialties, Inc.
Roanoke Council of Garden Clubs,
    Inc.
Roanoke County Education
    Association
Roanoke Education Association, Inc.
Roanoke Forms & Labels, Inc.
Roanoke Gas Company
Roanoke Network for Professional and
    Managerial Women
Roanoke Obstetrics & Gynecology, Inc.
Roanoke Orthopaedic Center
Roanoke Orthopedic Appliance
    Company
Roanoke Rails
Roanoke Regional Chamber of
    Commerce
Roanoke Regional Home Builders
    Association, Inc.
Roanoke Restaurant Service, Inc.
Roanoke Times & World News
Roanoke Valley Association of Realtors
Roanoke Valley Breakfast Lions Club
The Roanoke Valley Development
    Corporation
Roanoke Valley Medical Clinic, Inc.
Roanoke Valley Preservation
    Foundation
Roanoke Valley Realty & Associates,
    Inc.
Roanoke Valley Region Antique Auto
Rotary Club of the Roanoke Valley
Rotary Club of Roanoke-Downtown
Royal Publishing Company
RSM Enterprises, Inc.
S & H Auto Service
S & S Cafeterias
Salem Rotary Club
Salem Times-Register
Sam's on the Market, Inc.
Sarber Management Services
Scottish Society of the Virginia
    Highlands
Serv-N-Save, Inc.
Sewell Products, Inc.
SFCS
Shenandoah Industrial Rubber

Company
Shenanigans
Signet Bank Roanoke
Signet Trust Company
Singer Furniture Company
Skyline Cleaners, Inc.
Smith Mountain Dock, Inc.
Southern Title Insurance Corporation
Southwest Construction, Inc.
Southwest Virginia Savings Bank, FSB
Southwind, Ltd.
Spencer & Associates, PC
SPM Corporation
SRO Productions, Inc.
State Office Supply, Inc.
Strauss Construction Corporation
Summerell Company, Inc.
Swartz Restaurant Supply, Inc.
Sysco Food Services of Virginia, Inc.
Szechuan Restaurant
Tanglewood Breakfast Lions Club
Tanglewood Rental Management
Tate Sewing Center
Thomas Brothers, Inc.
Thomas P. Murphy, Inc.
Thomas Rutherfoord, Inc.
Thompson Masonry Contractors, Inc.
Timber Truss Housing Systems, Inc.
Time Technologies, Inc.
Tinaglia Real Estate, Inc.
Travel Professionals, Inc.
Travelmasters, Inc
Tread Corporation
Triquest FTD
Truck Sales, Inc.
Valley Cadillac Oldsmobile, Inc.
Valley Pathology Associates
Vesper Hill Developers
Veterinarians to Cats, Ltd.
Video Records, Inc.
The Vinton Messenger
Vinton Motor Company, Inc.
Virginia Building Services of Roanoke
Virginia Data Products, Inc.
Virginia Hair Academy
Virginia Housing Development
    Authority
Virginia Plastics Company, Inc.
Virginia Prosthetics, Inc.
Virginia Truck Center, Inc.
Virginia Valve Company
W. B. Clements, Inc.
W. S. Connelly & Company, Inc.
W. W. Boxley & Company
Waldvogel, Poe & Cronk
Warsaw Health Care Center
Waste Management of Virginia-Blue
    Ridge
WDBJ
Weaver, Weaver, Vascik & Kleiner
Wertz & Williams, Ltd.
Wertz's Country Store, Inc.
West Motor Sales

Western Sizzlin' Steak House
WFIR/WPVR
WFXR-TV Fox 27/WJPR-TV Fox 21
Wheat First Securities, Inc.
Wheaton Plumbing & Heating Company
Wheeler's Fast Service
Whitescarver, Hurd & Obenchain, Inc.
Williams Memorial Park, Inc.
Williams Supply, Inc.
Williamson Road Woman's Club
Woman's Club of Roanoke, Inc.
Woods, Rogers & Hazelgrove
Wooten & Hart, PC
Wright Business Machine, Inc.
WROV AM/FM
WSLC/WSLQ
WSLS
Yesteryear Hearts & Baskets
Yokohama Tire Company

Individuals

Thomas A. & Josephine M. Abbott
Mr. Jack M. Abell
Ms. Carol F. Adams
Mrs. Deborah H. Adams
Miss Reba A. Adams
T. Donald & Josephine B. Adams
Thomas H. & Jeanette G. Adams
Mr. George S. Agee
Philip L. & Anna G. Agee
Michael J. & Avis Lee Aheron
Ms. Ellen Aiken
T. B. Aird III & A. Marie Aird
Mr. Andrew M. Airheart
Andrew J. Airheart, Jr. & Sara S. Airheart
Mr. Hiromitsu Akashi
Mr. H. H. Akers
Ms. Sandra B. Akers
Michael M. & Vicki L. Akers
H. James Akers, Jr. & Ruth D. Akers
Mr. Rudolf F. Albert
Ms. Eva S. Aldhizer
J. V. & Grace S. Alexander
Mr. John A. Allen
Dr. John T. Allen
J. S. Allison
Ms. Ginny Allison
C. Bradie & Beverly H. Allman
R. L. & Joyce C. Allman
Roy G. & Lorraine R. Allman
Raymond T. Alouf, Sr. & Gail O. Alouf
Mrs. J. Ring Altizer
Mr. George D. Altizier
Robert L. Amick, Jr. & Nancy P. Amick
Norman A. & Trudy L. Andersen
Anthony F. & Uneita R. Anderson
Ms. Brenda W. Anderson
Mr. Paul P. Anderson
Mr. Willis M. Anderson
Don H. & Wendy M. Andree

Dr. Sandra Andrew
Mr. Briggs W. Andrews
Dr. Nancy A. Andrews
Stanley B. & Sharon B. Andrzejewski
H. Glenn & Lucille C. Angle
Ms. Judith L. Angle
Anonymous (several donors)
Ms. Anne Armistead
Miss Mary B. Armistead
Ms. Connie F. Armstrong
Ms. Tommy Arnold
E. B. & Jewel P. Arrington
Mr. Kenneth R. Arritt, Jr.
Steve L. & Norma Arthur
Ms. Edith O. Ashby
Robert L. & Judith J. Ashcraft
Ms. Norma N. Atchley
Ms. E. Lynn Atkinson
Ms. Velma M. Atkinson
Mr. Wendell G. Atkinson
James E. Atkinson, Jr. & Jule W. Atkinson
Mr. Joseph H. Austin
Joseph L. & Becky D. Austin
Ms. Katherine M. Austin
Mr. & Mrs. Dennis U. Austin, Jr.
Dr. Ted G. Avner
Mr. Charles W. Ayling
Mr. Edgar M. Baber
Mr. Cecil C. Baecher
Paul D. & Anne R. Bailey
Ms. Phyllis C. Bailey
Mr. Stephen R. Bailey
Dr. Dewey J. Bailey, Jr.
Mr. Billie L. Baines
Barry W. & Alison Baird
Mr. Cliff Baker
Ms. Margaret R. Baker
Mr. & Mrs. Ralph K. Baker, Jr.
Mr. & Mrs. Duke Baldridge III
Gary W. & Dot Baldwin
William B. & Marga L. Bales
Mr. Michael Ballantyne
Wade H. Ballard III & Val J. Ballard
F. Jackson & Winifred C. Ballenger
Ernest W. & Ruth S. Ballou
Mr. Robert S. Ballou
Mr. Jeffrey K. Bandy
John P. & Mildred P. Banks
Ms. Barbara Rowe Barbour
Thomas J. & Elizabeth E. Barila
Charles F. Barnett, Jr. & Virginia L. Barnett
Don & Sheila C. Barnhart
Harold E. & Louise R. Barron
Mr. Bruce A. Bartmess
Donald & Nan T. Bartol
Vincent T. & Mary Z. Basile
Ms. Linda S. Bass
Mr. & Mrs. William R. Battle
William R. Baumgardner, Jr. & Judith M.
    Baumgardner
Ms. Betty J. Bauserman
Ms. Elizabeth Baybutt
T. Richard Beard, Jr. & Susan W. Beard

Mr. Howard J. Beck, Jr.
Mr. Alfred Beckley
Ms. Gloria D. Beckner
J. L. & Pauline D. Beckner
Ms. Robin Beckner
Ms. Lu Jean Bedard
Mr. R. T. Beedie
James W. & Sharon A. Behrens
Mr. William S. Bell
Mr. Houston L. Bell, Jr.
James J. & Beverly K. Bendel
Albert D. & Jane H. Bender
Ms. Laura E. Benjamin
Robert & Shirley G. Berbert
Thompson & Doris M. Berdeen
Mrs. Margie D. Berger
Mr. Thomas C. Berger
Beverley Berkeley, Jr. & Anne B. Berkeley
Dr. Robert E. Berry
Ms. Sarah M. Berry
Timothy B. & Linda B. Berry
Mr. Robert S. Bersch
E. R. & Shirley Biggs
Warren L. & Laura C. Bingham
Robert H. & Ann D. Bird
Ms. Carol S. Birmingham
Mr. Ragan L. Bishop
Carl H. & Mary Bivens
Mr. Delaney C. Black
Mr. Mark Black
Dr. James E. Blackwell
Mr. & Mrs. S. Wilson Blain
Mr. W. Edward Blain
William E. Blandford II & Jennifer N. Blandford
Mr. J. P. Blankenship
R. Jerry & Lucy K. Blankenship
Douglas D. & Suzanne M. Blevins
Dr. F. D. Bloss
Ronald D. & Kay G. Blum
Gwynn H. & Eileen P. Board & Family
Martin H. & Rachel C. Bocock
T. J. & Beverly W. Boehling
Mr. H. Preston Boggess
Malcolm C. & Jean M. Boggs
Mr. Howard W. Boise, Jr.
Ms. Kitty J. Boitnott
Mr. Orlin Boitnott
Mr. & Mrs. W. Chan Bolling
Dr. & Mrs. Robert F. Bondurant
Mr. Barry L. Booher
Ms. Evelyn W. Booker
Mr. Daniel E. Boone
Leonard C. & Georgia O. Borland
Graham H. & Carrie R. Bourhill
Ms. Nancy A. Bourne
Mr. Richard D. Boush
Ms. Nancy R. Bower
Mr. David A. Bowers
Homer A. & Mary A. Bowers
Mr. & Mrs. Ralph K. Bowles
E. Glenn & Helen T. Bowman
Mrs. Abney Boxley, Jr.
Mr. Frank A. Boxley, Jr.

Abney S. Boxley III & Martha B. Boxley
Ms. Lillian G. Boyer
Mrs. Sadie M. Boyle
William D. Brackman, Jr. & Carole U. Brackman
Ms. Betty T. Bradshaw
Mr. & Mrs. Robert L. Bradshaw, Jr.
Mrs. William Brady
David F. & Ravenelle L. Brammer
Ms. Mignon R. Brammer
Mr. & Mrs. Cabell Brand
Ms. Kathleen H. Brantley
Ms. Carolyn M. Bratton
Dr. & Mrs. Charles B. Bray
Stanley & Edith Breakell
Mrs. Muriel E. Bredlow
Ms. Louisa H. Breeden
Mrs. M. P. Breeden
S. G. & Pamela W. Breeding
Warren M. & Emma S. Brickhouse
Mr. & Mrs. Paul N. Bridge
Mr. & Mrs. J. Phil Briggs
Ms. Marilyn V. Brigham
Mr. John A. Bright
Ms. S. G. Bright
Roy I. & Robin Brindle
Mr. Jon P. Brisley
William C. & Jacquelyn B. Britts
Henry T. & Muriel H. Brobst
Dr. Susan R. Brooker-Gross
Carlton P. & Cynthia S. Brooks
John & Beth Brooks
Mr. Arnold W. Brown
Mrs. D.B. Brown
Mr. Daniel S. Brown
Mr. John E. Brown
Ms. Martha B. Brown
Mrs. Mary-Margaret B. Brown
Mr. H. Cletus Broyles
Ms. Jean M. Broyles
Herman W. & Hazel F. Brubaker
William S. Bruce, Jr. & Mary Lou Bruce
Ms. Kae A. Bruch
Mr. Bud Brumitt
Ms. Marie W. Bryan
Ms. Linda M. Bryant
Mr. Richard L. Bryant
Robert E. & Judy B. Bryant
Ms. Kathryn K. Buchanan
Ms. Mary Alice M. Buchanan
Ms. Sue Buchanan
Mr. Geo J. Buchanan, Jr.
Jamie B. & Debbie H. Buckland
Mr. Joseph B. Buhrman
Bill & Paula L. Bumgarner
Dr. Patricia P. Bundy
Mr. Carter L. Burgess
Mrs. Janice K. Burks
Jack M. & Nannette P. Burnett
Mr. John W. Burress, III
Mrs. Betty J. Burrows
Mr. David H. Burrows
Mr. W. Jackson Burrows

Mr. E. D. Burtis
Ms. Ann M. Burton
Mrs. Virginia E. Burton
W. Frank Burton, Jr. & Grace H. Burton
Joseph L. & Mary C. Bush
Mr. Gilbert E. Butler
John J. & Jane D. Butler
Ms. June N. Butler
Mr. Gilbert E. Butler, Jr.
Mr. John W. Butterfield
Mr. A. Dale Byington
Ms. Nancy M. Cabaniss
Mrs. Beatrice W. Caldwell
Ms. Nancy L. Caldwell
Stoke G. & Rosemary Caldwell
John D. & Lisa C. Calhoun
Ms. Barbara A. Calnan
Ms. Nancy L. Calvert
G. Keen & Dorothy S. Campbell
Mrs. Gertrude C. Campbell
Mr. Raleigh Campbell
Mr. S. Wayne Campbell
Mr. Warren B. Campbell
Rhudy & Cathryn P. Camper
Ms. Catherine J. Cannady
Mr. J. Richard Carling
Mrs. Henry F. Carmack
R. Wayne & Judith S. Carman
Mr. Paul A. Carmichael
Mrs. EllaSue W. Carr
Mrs. Irene W. Carr
Mr. J. Mark Carr
Mr. William F. Carson
Robert D. Carson, Jr. & Sandra G. Carson
Ms. Shirley H. Carter
Mr. & Mrs. W. James Carter, Jr.
William P. Carter, Jr. & Phyllis A. Carter
Larry S. & Charlotte L. Carver
Mrs. Ann R. Cassell
Mr. Domenic B. Castellane
Dr. Louis J. Castern
David L. & Cynthia H. Caudill
Roy E. & Dorothy S. Caudill
C. Dennis & Marcine H. Causey
Mr. James B. Cavendish
Dr. Ranes C. Chakravorty
Ms. Alice P. Chambers
Mrs. Mary B. Chambers
Ms. Jane E. Chance
Mr. John M. Chaney, Jr.
Jerry & Jane D. Cheadle
Ms. Joan Y. Childress
Mr. & Mrs. H. J. Childress, Jr.
Ms. Geraldine P. Chivas
Ms. Spring Cho
J. W. & Jane Christenbury
Mr. J. W. Christenbury, Jr.
Michael W. & Barbara A. Cisco
G. E. & Mary W. Clapsaddle
Mr. C. Mack Clark
Jeffrey D. & Lynn R. Clark
Kim S. & Bonnie H. Clark
Lewis D. & Edna C. Clark

Richard L. & Judith W. Clark
Mr. William F. Clark
Ms. Louise R. Clarke
Joseph M. Clarke II & Vickie R. Clarke
Ms. Catherine H. Clem
G. O. & Patricia L. Clemens
G. Frank & Evelyn R. Clement
Mr. William F. Clement
Miss Sarah L. Clendenen
Orrin W. & Dorothy S. Clifton
Stephen P. & Elaine A. Clinton
Mr. & Mrs. W. N. Cochran
Mr. Jerry T. Cock
Mr. Edgar M. Cocke
Dr. & Mrs. E. L. Coffey
Dr. John Cole, Jr.
Mr. W. Patton Coles IV
Dr. Beth A. Collins
Robert G. & Amy M. Collins
Mrs. L. Preston Collins III
Mr. Bobby J. Combs
Glen C. & Marsha Combs
W. P. & Jeanette H. Combs
Mr. William E. Comer
Dr. Charles E. Conklin, Jr.
Ms. Beverly W. Conley
Herbert C. Conley III & Joyce E. Conley
Mr. S. Richard Conner
Mr. Robert S. Conte
Mrs. D. Herrick Cook
Miss Marie Cook
Mr. Paul S. Cooper
Robert M. & Belle N. Cooper
Mr. Robert M. Cooper, Jr.
Dr. & Mrs. R. T. Copenhaver
Daniel P. Corey, Jr. & Anne M. Corey
Mr. Joe Corne
Ms. Terri L. Cornwell
Ms. Pauline J. Corso
Ms. Linda L. Cory
James G. & Noel B. Cosby
Mr. Louis R. Coulling, Jr.
Judge & Mrs. Jack B. Coulter
Mr. Philip C. Coulter
Mrs. Mary Anne Coulter
Mr. & Mrs. W. Albert Coulter
William J. & Iris C. Council
Mr. John E. Cowhig
Ms. Anne B. Cox
Howard T. & Margaret T. Cox
Ms. Lois Ann Cox
Mr. Woodrow H. Cox
Mrs. Robert M. Cox, Jr.
Mr. Charles D. Cox III
Hugh & Regina Craft
Ms. Betty C. Craig
Mr. Harry T. Craig
Gary W. & Karen Crawford
Mr. Gordon W. Crawford
R. B. & C. K. Crawford
Thomas J. & Ann Crawford
Mrs. Adelaide S. Creasy
Mr. John W. Creasy

Lewis A. & Dorothy T. Creasy
Dr. R. S. Creekmore
Frank A. & Susan B. Cregger
Dr. & Mrs. Charles L. Crockett, Jr.
Carl S. & Mary Jane Cross
Charles W. Crosson, Jr. and Margaret W. Crosson
Ms. Hazel C. Crowder
Dr. Junius E. Crowgey
Mr. Terence H. Crowgey
Mr. & Mrs. Douglas Cruickshanks, Jr.
E. P. & Helen Crumpler, Sr.
Ms. Virginia O. Crutchfield-Sherertz
John S. & Martha D. Crute
C. William Cubberley, Jr. & Barbara J. Cubberley
Buck & Sharron Cullop
Kenneth D. & Linda R. Cumins
Edward R. & B. V. Cundiff
Gregory D. & Marjorie L. Cundiff
Chesley C. & Martha S. Cunningham
Robert & Bette S. Cunningham
Mr. Robert Q. Cunningham
Tom & Eleanor G. Cunningham
J. T. Cunningham III & Jane R. Cunningham
Dr. M. Rupert Cutler
Ms. Doris W. Cutright
Dr. Anthony D. Cuzzocrea
Ms. Mary A. Dalby
Mr. A. Paul Dallas
Ms. C. Naomi Dalon
Mr. Hugh F. Dalton, Jr.
Mr. David J. Damico
Ms. Jane K. Daniel
Vern & Carol Danielsen
Mrs. Helen B. Danner
John F. & Julie M. Danstrom
Ms. Jean K. Darby
Ms. Mary H. Darden
Henry A. Davenport, Jr. & Marie Davenport
Sigmund E. & Harriet C. Davidson
Mr. Peter V. Davies II
Mr. & Mrs. Billie H. Davis
Ms. Elizabeth Y. Davis
Gene A. & Velma V. Davis
J. W. & Alice Davis
James P. & Peggy C. Davis
Mr. Philip P. Davis
Ronald E. & Elizabeth W. Davis
Mr. & Mrs. Thomas E. Davis
Mrs. Virginia I. Davis
Mr. Curtis E. Davis, Jr.
Philip E. & Jean B. Day
Mr. Placido H. DeGuzman
Dr. John P. Delaney
Mr. H. Michael Deneka
Douglas F. & Sue P. DePuy
Mr. Mark H. Derbyshire
Mr. E. L. Derring
Dr. Jitendra Desai
Mr. John S. DeVerter
Mr. Walter L. DeWitt
Mrs. Dorothy Deyerle

Dr. William A. Deyerle
Dr. & Mrs. William J. Dichtel
Mr. S. C. Dickerson
Dr. Walter H. Dickey
Mrs. Barbara M. Dickinson
Mr. W. A. Dickinson
Mr. W. Andrew Dickinson, Jr.
Harold F. Dill, Jr. & Elizabeth C. Dill
Mr. Michael W. Dillon
Mr. Walter M. Dixon
G. Wayne & Jean B. Dodson
Jerry & Melinda Doggett
Mr. Robert P. Doherty, Jr.
Mr. Laura J. Dolinger
Ms. Janice S. Dominick
Dr. Antonio T. Donato
Ms. Norma L. Donelson
Barry L. & Virginia R. Dooley
Mrs. Dorothy L. Dooley
Mr. Earl D. Doran
David R. & Katherine E. Dougherty
Mrs. Helen B. Douglas
Mrs. Melva J. Dowdy
Mr. Perry R. Downing
Dr. Charles L. Downs
Mrs. Hazel J. Drain
Mr. L. Crozier Draper
Ms. Margaret W. Dressler
Mr. & Mrs. Wilbur A. Drewery
Ms. Margaret C. Drewry
Ms. Pearl M. Drewry
Mrs. William E. Driscoll
Mr. Kevin F. Ducey
F. Joseph & Sharon G. Duckwall
John M. & Elizabeth N. Duckworth
Dr. Frank H. Dudley
S. Cabell & Libba Dudley
Larry D. Dudley, Sr. & Evelyn B. Dudley
Mr. & Mrs. G. R. Duerk
Robert G. Duggar, Jr. & Cynthia K. Duggar
Ms. Katharine J. Dunavan
Mr. Edward C. Dunbar
Ms. Louise Dunlap
Mr. J. Melvin Dunman
Ms. Betty G. Durham
George J. & Florence Durmann
Mr. Dennis D. Durrette
Mr. David Duschean
Mr. & Mrs. Joseph J. Duschean, Jr.
Mr. Chuck Dyson
Mr. William M. Dyson
Ronald E. & Judy B. East
Mr. Frank Eastburn
William G. & Tommye C. Eddins
Ms. Frances B. Eddy
Mr. Lee B. Eddy
Guido A. & Shirley W. Edillon
Ms. Dorothy L. Edwards
Mr. J. Randolph Edwards
Mr. & Mrs. B. Purnell Eggleston
Ms. Patricia J. Ekdahl
Ms. Peggy Eller
Walter A. & Patricia Ellinghausen

Samuel E. & Dora Lee Ellington
Ms. Anne W. Elliott
Mr. Bruce D. Elliott
H. W. & Bertie K. Elliott
Ms. Marilyn K. Elliott
Mr. U. Wayne Elliott
Mr. Eugene M. Elliott, Jr.
George T. & Josephine G. Ellis
Mr. & Mrs. Henry G. Ellis
Louis E. & Rebecca E. Ellis
Ms. Mae D. Ellis
Norman E. & Lucille W. Elmore
Mr. W. H. Engle
Mr. Paul M. English
Ms. Doris N. Ennis
Mr. Frank Epperly
William R. & Patricia J. Erwin
John W. & Peggy T. Eure
Mr. James B. Evans
Mr. F. H. Ewald
Edwin J. & Jane M. Ewing
Mrs. Lynne P. Falkinburg
Dr. Newell R. Falkinburg
Randall K. & Kathleen L. Falls
Ms. Annie P. Fancher
Dr. Steven L. Farber
Mr. & Mrs. Frank A. Farmer, Jr.
Ms. Jane B. Farnum
Thomas W. & Connie L. Farrell
Edwin R. & Susan M. Feinour
Dr. Bernard F. Feldman
Gregory W. & Elizabeth T. Feldmann
Mark E. & Whitney H. Feldmann
Mr. Gary N. Fenton
Ms. Patricia D. Ferguson
Mr. Robert H. Fetzer
H. Otto & Jeanette M. Feuer
Mr. William W. Field, Jr.
Ms. Dorothy S. Findlay
J. Robert Finton, Jr. & Joanna H. Finton
Mr. Benny Firestone
George K. Fischer, Jr. & Peggy A. Fischer
Dennis G. & Glenna E. Fisher
Hugh C. & Catherine B. Fisher
Ms. Margie R. Fisher
Dr. & Mrs. R. H. Fisher
Richard H. & Adelaide L. Fisher
John P. & Doreen M. Fishwick
Ms. Grace T. Fitzgerald
Lem Fitzgerald, Sr. & Catherine Fitzgerald
Broaddus & Luann M. Fitzpatrick
Mrs. Earl A. Fitzpatrick
Mr. Eric E. Fitzpatrick
Mr. B. T. Fitzpatrick, Jr.
Mr. B. T. Fitzpatrick III
Judge Beverly T. Fitzpatrick, Sr. & Helen
    C. Fitzpatrick
Mr. & Mrs. William H. Flannagan
Jack W. & Beatrice L. Fleshman
Mr. & Mrs. G. F. Flippin
Carl B. & Leola B. Flora
Ms. Donna J. Flora
Frederick W. & Sandra K. Flowers
Ms. Barbara S. Fogel
Al & Edna W. Follmar
Mr. James A. Ford

William C. & Sally B. Foreman
David L. & Joyce M. Foster
Ms. Natalie R. Foster
Ralph O. & Barbara S. Foster
William G. & Joanne M. Foster
Ms. Catherine A. Fox
Ms. Ethel C. Fralin
Mr. William H. Fralin, Jr.
Eddie R. & Mabel M. France
Robert K. France & Ruth A. Doan
Mr. C. W. Francis & Son
Ms. Margaret E. Francis
John R. Francis, Jr. & Rosemary D. Francis
C. Gilbert & Susan C. Frank
Ms. Vivian Frank
Dr. Walter R. Franke
Mr. J. Stuart Franklin, Jr.
Mr. James S. Frantz
Paul M. & Josephine T. Frantz
Dr. Paul T. Frantz
Mr. Tommy Frantz
Mrs. Betty F. Freeman
Dr. John D. French
Ms. Gerlinde H. Friedewald
T. Daniel Frith III & Linda D. Frith
Mark A. & Lynne K. Frye
Mr. S. L. Fulcher
Ms. Frances S. Fulghum
Mr. James H. Fulghum, Jr.
Miss Dorothea M. Fuller
Ms. Dorothea R. Fuller
Ms. Penny J. Fulton
Ms. Sally F. Fulton
Dale S. & Joan B. Furbish
Mr. David M. Furman
Ms. Pam M. Gacek
Dr. James C. Gale
Ms. Emma F. Gallimore
Dr. Ray W. Gandee
Dr. Jorge M. Garcia
Frank T. & Virginia E. Garden
Dr. James P. Gardner, Jr.
Reginald W. & Glenna G. Garner
Mr. Lee Garrett
Mr. Olin Garrett
Robert G. Garrett, Jr. & Alice C. Garrett
Mr. & Mrs. Jack R. Garrison
Ms. Martha M. Garrison
Mr. Tim Garrison
Ms. Judy E. Garst
Mr. Paul H. Garst
Mr. Hugh C. Garth
Ms. Myrtle I. Gartman
Mrs. Lois B. Gaunt
Mr. G. William Gearhart
G. W. Gearhart, Jr. & Dianne B. Gearhart
John T. & Leria B. Geary
Ms. Kathleen M. Genaitis
Mr. W. Fred Genheimer III
Mr. & Mrs. William F. George
Ms. Louise S. Gibson
Mr. Thomas D. Gibson
Tom & Joyce J. Gibson
Dr. Carol M. Gilbert
Warren W. & Hassie Gilbert
Ms. Evelyn G. Giles

Mr. Richard M. Giles, Jr.
Mrs. Mary L. S. Gillespie
Dr. Charles D. Gilliland
Mr. & Mrs. Donald L. Gilmer
Ms. Rita P. Gilmore
Mr. R. Michael Gilmore
Peter S. & Carole G. Givens
Dr. Jean M. Glasgow
Harold C. & Elizabeth B. Glass
Mr. & Mrs. Henry Gleixner
Ms. Lucy D. Glenn
Mr. Rob Glenn
Ms. Hannah T. Glisson
Ms. Debra L. Glovier
Edward P. & Suzanne G. Godsey
Ms. Gail G. Godsey
Mr. Gerald W. Godsey
Mr. Jerry Godsey
Bernard E. & Nancy L. Goehring
Nathan W. & Sally E. Goff
R. Grayson & Eva Goldsmith
Andrew S. & Adrienne Bloss Goldstein
Garrett G. Gooch III & Anne H. Gooch
Michael R. & Katherine H. Good
Mr. David R. Goode
Dr. James J. Gooding
Robert W. & Maryellen F. Goodlatte
Ms. Joyce L. Goodwin
Edward L. & Deanna W. Gordon
Robert & Rosemary Goss
Ms. Sue Gotwalt
Mr. W. Clyde Grasty
Mr. James D. Gravely
Gary W. & Stormy L. Gray
Mr. Farnum Gray, Jr.
Jack R. Graybill, Jr. & Louise Graybill
Dr. Richard J. Grayson, Jr.
Mr. James P. Green
Mr. Kossen Gregory
John Gregory, Jr. & Tallulah H. Gregory
Mrs. Blanche G. Griffin
Ms. Virginia D. Griffin
Mr. & Mrs. Donald L. Grisso
Mr. James D. Grisso
Robert M. & Mary M. Groth
Mr. Lucian Y. Grove
Mr. Jerry W. Grubb
Ms. Susan Grubb
Mr. Kurt W. Guelzow
Mr. Jack Guffey
Mr. Curtis E. Guilliams
Ms. Loleta Guilliams
Ms. Elizabeth Gulyas
Marvin & Joseph G. Gunselman
Mrs. Evelyn Gunter
Mr. James B. Gurley
Alton L. Gwaltney, Jr. & Jacqueline L.
    Gwaltney
Walter C. Gwaltney, Jr. & Mary P. Gwaltney
Mr. Mark D. Gwin
Mr. J. Bruce Hagadorn
Ms. Alice T. Hagan
William C. & Nancy P. Hagan
G. Ronald & Andrea M. Hager
J. A. & Carol Hagy
John W. & L. Dale Hahn

Mr. Hassell A. Hale
R. Richard Hale, Jr. & Tammy T. Hale
Ms. Andrea Haley
Duncan K. & Jane W. Haley
Mrs. Virginia M. Hall
Mr. W. E. Hall
Mrs. Wannie S. Hall
Dr. Kenneth L. Hallman
Mr. & Mrs. A. C. Halsey
Al & Cheryl B. Ham
Mrs. Anne B. Hammersley
Robert A. & Jennifer L. Hammersley
Ms. Donna M. Hamner
Dr. Mark R. Hanabury, Jr.
Ms. Carolyn C. Hancock
Mrs. Diane C. Hancock
Mr. Philip T. Hand
Mr. Phillip A. Hanood, Jr.
Ms. Jeannine B. Hanson
Ms. Helen P. Hardy
J. A. & Helen W. Hardy
Ms. Ruth Hardy
Ms. Phyllis V. Harholdt
Mr. James W. Harkness
W. R. Harp, Jr. & Jean C. Harp
Mr. & Mrs. Kenneth E. Harper
Mr. C. Jackson Harrill
Dr. Daniel P. Harrington
Ms. Audrey W. Harris
Ms. Clara E. Harris
Marshall, Nancy & Kim Harris
Dr. Ronald B. Harris
Ms. Alice W. Harrison
Ms. Carolyn Harrison
George F. & Rebecca Harrison
Ms. Judith A. Harrison
Howard O. Harrison, Jr. & Martha P. Harrison
William D. & Jeanne B. Hart
Jack E. & Josephine T. Hartfield
Mrs. Mary B. Hartley
Frank E. & Susan I. Hartman
Wesley T. & Sandra C. Hartman
Mr. Lee C. Hartman, Jr.
John E. & Jean F. Harvey
Ms. Gail P. Harwood
Ms. Melanie L. Haskins
Charles H. Hatcher III & Linda K. Hatcher
Mr. Stephen M. Hatchett
Dr. J. Bruce Hauser
Mr. Russell B. Hawkins II
Fred S. & Madelyn A. Hawks
Mrs. Elta R. Hayden
Ms. Francine Hayes
Robert B. & Jeannette D. Hayes
Mr. O. Bryan Hayes, Jr.
Raymond G. & Della J. Haymaker
Ms. Mary Haynes
Ms. Thelma Haynesworth
Ms. Kathryn B. Haynie
Mrs. Jos. W. Hazlegrove
Ms. Adrian C. Healy
Walker B. Healy, Jr. & Nancy R. Healy
Mr. Eddie F. Hearp
Roger A. & Linnae R. Hedgbeth
Dr. Charles A. Hefner
Ms. Kay Heidbreder

I. B. & Harriet S. Heinemann
Mrs. Victor A. Heiner
Mr. John G. Heitz
Mr. Robert A. Heller
Max M. Helms, Sr. & Mary D. Helms
William R. & Edith M. Hencke
Mr. Jamie R. Hendry
Miss Shirley E. Henn
George H. & Blanche H. Henning
Dr. Thomas R. & Johanna M. Henretta
Ms. Evelyn F. Hensley
Ms. Judith L. Hensley
Mr. W. Robert Herbert
Mr. Wayne Herkness II
Ms. Dianne M. Hernandez
Richard C. & Janice H. Herring
Mrs. Martha E. Hesser
Mr. F. Staley Hester, Jr.
Ms. Mary Lou Hiatt
Mr. Michael Hiatt
Mr. Byron A. Hicks
Mr. Michael R. Hicks
W. Vernon & Lucille K. Hicks
Ms. Martha B. Higginbotham
Mr. Donald L. Hill
Ms. Jane M. Hill
Mr. Larry R. Hill
O. Halsey & Emily B. Hill
Paul C. & Georgia P. Hill
Cecil L. Hill, Sr. & Wanda L. Hill
Ms. Mary W. Hilliard
Karen K. & Dennis P. Hilson
Mr. & Mrs. William P. Hilts
Ms. Jean S. Himes
Mr. Ernest C. Hinck III
Dr. John L. Hines
Ms. Mary E. Hinman
Ms. Virginia B. Hinman
Ms. Patricia A. Hinneburg
Mr. Charles A. Hite III
Ms. Hazel E. Hoback
Ms. Elizabeth C. Hobbie
Mr. J. Dexter Hobbie III
Elmer C. Hodge, Jr. & Alice R. Hodge
B. Larry & Judy B. Hodges
Ms. Mimi Hodgin
Mr. Robert W. Hoel
Joseph M. & Lillian E. Hoer
Mr. Christian A. Hoeser
Mr. Carl J. Hoffman
Mr. F. Courtney Hoge
Ms. Helen Hoge
Ms. Charlotte W. Holcomb
Marvin E. & Laura C. Holcombe
E. W. & Reva T. Holland
Mr. James R. Holland
Ms. Shirley B. Holland
Mr. Donald E. Holliday, Jr.
Dr. J. Hayden Hollingsworth
James C. Hollins, Jr. & Emily P. Hollins
Mr. Gerald A. Holm
Dr. James F. Holman
Mr. W. Jefferson Holt
Ms. Phyllis Holton
Mr. Horace Hood III
William E. & Kelly B. Hooper

Stephen A. & Jane B. Hoover
Mr. Fortescue W. Hopkins
Mr. M. Marshall Hopkins
Mrs. J. Thomas Hopkins, Jr.
Mr. James T. Hopkins III
Mrs. Caroline M. Horne
Mr. & Mrs. Robert R. Horner, Jr.
Mr. Raymond D. Horton
William R. & Rebecca B. Houchins
William B. Houck, Jr. & Katherine F. Houck
R. Franklin Hough, Jr. & Jane L. Hough
Jerome S. Howard, Jr. & Jane S. Howard
Mr. James E. Howell
Mr. Paul M. Howell
Mr. & Mrs. W. Stebbins Hubard, Jr.
William S. Hubard, Sr. & Elizabeth J. Hubard
Mr. F. Wiley Hubbell
Mr. Stewart W. Hubbell
Ms. Karen R. Hudgins
Bertrand R. Hudnall II & Martha D. Hudnall
Mr. Thomas M. Hudson
Clayton H. Hudson, Jr. & Hope H. Hudson
Leigh P. Huff, Jr. & Anne T. Huff
Ms. Anne H. Huffman
Ms. Lois J. Huffman
Maynard D. & Denise R. Huffman
Ms. Carol B. Hughes
Dr. William H. Humphries, Jr.
Mr. Frank E. Humston
Mr. David S. Hunt
Keith K. & Mary L. Hunt
Mr. Robert H. Hunt
Keith K. Hunt, Jr. & Carmelita H. Hunt
Ms. Margaret S. Hunter
William T. & Sidney Y. Hunter
Mr. & Mrs. Charles E. Hunter, Jr.
Donald C. & Irene D. Hurley
Mr. Everett R. Hurst
Dr. A. J. Hurt
Mr. Calvin C. Hurt
Ms. Jean M. Hurt
John E. & Kathryn S. Husted
Mr. Reginald K. Hutcherson
Jack R. Hutcheson, Jr. & Charlene D. Hutcheson
Dr. & Mrs. Robert S. Hutcheson, Jr.
Mr. John M. Hylton
Mrs. Roy L. Hylton
Ms. Nancy J. Ingram
Dr. Lowell F. Inhorn
Mr. R. Jay Irons
Dr. Robert W. Irvin, Jr.
Mr. William A. Irvin, Jr.
William A. Irvin III & Robbie P. Irvin
Mr. Robert F. Iseminger, Jr.
Ms. J. S. Isgrig
Ms. Linda T. Ives
Mr. & Mrs. W. Bolling Izard
Peter W. & Mary W. Jackson
Ms. Melanie L. Jacobs
A. M. & Ruth P. Jacobson
Ms. Beverly A. James
Mr. Bruce W. Janney
Mr. & Mrs. R. Devereux Jarratt
Dallas G. & Joyce H. Jarrell
Dr. William E. Jefferson III

Ross E. & Janet M. Jeffries
Harold F. & Frances M. Jennings
Mr. E. Fitzgerald Jennings, Jr.
Carl S. & Carol W. Jensen
John & Lee Jessee
Ms. Mildred C. Jofko
Boyd & Barbara Johnson
Ms. Diane W. Johnson
Ms. Helen T. Johnson
Mr. James M. Johnson
Jim F. & Mary Ann H. Johnson
John P. & Shirley S. Johnson
Ms. Kathryn A. Johnson
Ms. Mickey Johnson
Ms. Mildred I. Johnson
Richard L. & Ava Gwen Johnson
Mr. Robert S. Johnson
William W. & Ann Jones Johnson
William W. & Becky L. Johnson
Mr. & Mrs. Harry G. Johnson, Jr.
Mr. R. W. Johnson, Jr.
Rodell C. Johnson, Jr. & Suzanne C. Johnson
Mr. Wesley T. Johnson, Jr.
Mr. Pegramm Johnson III
Conrad & Louise P. Jones
Dr. Daniel R. Jones
Harold R. & Virginia J. Jones
J. David & Karen H. Jones
James E. & Shirley W. Jones
Mr. Robert Jones
Mr. Thomas B. Jones
Mr. Reid Jones, Jr.
Howard Jones, Sr. & Sharon Y. Jones
Mr. Mark S. Journell
Ms. Karon G. Joyner
Mr. David A. Justis
Dr. William J. Kagey
Mr. Roger D. Kahle
Paul F. & Susan H. Kaiser
Ms. Ruth E. Kaminester
Mr. Stanley B. Kamm
Y. S. & Elizabeth R. Kang
Mr. Andrew F. Kaplan
Ms. Robin T. Karim
Ms. Roslyn W. Katz
Dr. John P. Kaufman
Richard B. & Janice H. Kaufman
R. L. A. & Nina B. Keeley
Donald W. & Diane P. Kees
Mr. George A. Kegley
Mr. & Mrs. George F. Kelch
Mr. Brian A. Kelley
Richard L. & Carol A. Kelley
Mrs. Edith H. Kelly
Dr. James A. Kelly
Ms. Patricia M. Kelly
Ms. Patricia P. Kelly
Timothy A. & Jane Kelly & Family
Mr. & Mrs. William W. Kelly
Dr. James C. Kemper
Ms. Kim B. Kennedy
Stephen S. & Marion Sue Kennedy
Ms. E. Claire Kennett
Jesse E. & Martha P. Kent
Charles & Gena Kepley
J. C. & Betty F. Kepley

Jack W. & Doris H. Kepner
Mr. James P. Kern
John R. & Sandra A. Kern
Miss Kathryn L. Kesler
Mr. W. J. Kesler
A. Reif & Susan B. Kessler
Mr. Maurice M. Kessler
Mr. Michael M. Kessler
Mr. Tommy W. Kessler
Mr. K. A. Key
Ms. M. Emily Keyser
Mr. Ali Yar Khan
Edward S. Kidd, Jr. & Betty Jo Kidd
Mr. Ed Kielty
Mr. Richmond W. Kienle
Edward J. & Joy L. Kilbane
Ms. Joann B. Kilcher
Franklin D. & Suzanne B. Kimbrough
Scott A. & Martha R. Kincaid
Mr. & Mrs. Ralph E. Kincer
James A. & Sara S. King
M. Frederick & Denise P. King
Stephen E. & Linda J. King
Ms. Vickie L. King
E. L. & Ruth C. Kingery
Mr. W. R. Kingery, Sr.
Rev. Dr. William E. Kinser
Mr. Gwynn Kinsey
Dr. David A. Kinsler
Elbert W. & Lillian P. Kinzie
Ms. Marguerite W. Kirk
Ms. Nettie L. Kitchen
Mr. R. Warren Kitts
Mr. John P. Klein
Dr. Lawrence I. Kleiner
Mr. Eugene W. Klick
Aubrey L. & Esther E. Knight
Mrs. Eleanor D. Knott
Drs. Michael H. & Mary Ann Koch
Mr. Douglas K. Kollme
Mr. & Mrs. Michael J. Kolnok, Jr.
Ms. Kathleen C. Koomen
Mr. Edward Korsh
Mr. Jeffrey H. Krasnow
Ms. Winifred S. Krasnow
Mrs. Eleanora B. Kraus
Mr. & Mrs. Allie B. Kreger, Jr.
Ms. Vicki C. Kreider
Ms. Gail B. Kreig
Drs. James M. & Linda S. Krell
Ms. Heidi Krisch
Roger W. & Kathleen M. Kronau
Robert A. & Mary Anne Kulp
Robert H. & Betty B. Kulp
Dr. and Mrs. Arthur A. Kunkle
Herbert S. & Gertrude Kurshan
Harold P. & Ann P. Kyle
Andrew J. & Margaret Lambert
Mr. Jackson M. Lambert
John W. Lambert, Jr. & Beverly B. Lambert
Dr. James N. Lampros
Mr. John N. Lampros
Dr. Leo N. Lampros
Brian K. & Laura M. Land
Mr. Harry E. Land
Virgil S. Lane, Jr. & Madora L. Lane

Mrs. Helen E. Lang
Dr. Miguel Langebeck
David G. & Gaynell M. Larsen
Ms. Hilda R. Larson
Ms. Karen Larson
Mr. E. W. Lautenschlager
Mr. & Mrs. William O. Lavin
Douglas L. & Dorothy B. Law
Dr. Maynard H. Law
David C. & Cindy Lawrence
Douglas B. & Sue D. Lawrence
Mr. Mark S. Lawrence
William J. & Wanda B. Lawrence
Mr. & Mrs. Joseph P. Lawson
Mr. Robert C. Lawson, Jr.
Clarence J. & Dorothy W. Layman
Mr. & Mrs. J. Allen Layman
Mr. Michael E. Layne
Mr. Lloyd G. Lazarus
Mr. William C. Leach
Thomas H. & Eleanor T. Leath
Mr. Robert G. Lee
Mr. Robert E. Lee, Jr.
Todd & Whitney Leeson
Mr. Charles L. Legg
C. Lawrence Legg, Jr. & Denise G. Legg
Charles R. & Anne L. Lemon
E. Marvin & Mary G. Lemon
Mr. Philip H. Lemon
Mr. Stephen W. Lemon
Mr. William J. Lemon
Mr. Charles F. Lerry
Dr. & Mrs. Edmund M. Lesko
Mr. Charles E. Leslie
Mr. & Mrs. Michael E. Levan
Mr. A. Bernard Levin
Mr. Burton Levine
Mr. Scott R. Leweke
Mr. & Mrs. A. W. Lewis
Mrs. Lois S. Lewis
Van L. & Ruth E. Lewis
Dr. Verna M. Lewis
Virgil E. & Lucille B. Lewis
Ms. Rosie LeFontaine
Mr. John E. Lichenstein
Ms. Charlotte T. Lichtenstein
Ms. Deborah Light-Liles
Mrs. Eula T. Ligon
Ms. Louisa B. Likens
Ms. Sue J. Lindsey
Mr. James R. Lindsey, Jr.
Mr. Samuel L. Lionberger, Jr.
Ms. Sue C. Lipscomb
David K. & Jean Lisk
Ernie & Debbie Littlefield
Ms. Angelica D. Lloyd
John H. & Rebecca C. Locke
L. Dorcas & Mabel R. Lofland
Alice C. & Charles I. Loftin
Mr. Charles M. Logan
Mr. George W. Logan
Joseph D. Logan III & Laura B. Logan
Mr. Gary R. Long
Mr. & Mrs. Samuel B. Long
Bobby C. & Jane C. Looney
Mr. Don Lorton

Dr. Christopher M. Lothes
Ms. Elizabeth A. Lotochinski
Ms. Frances Lotochinski
Mr. James M. Lotochinski
Mr. & Mrs. Marvin N. Lougheed
Mr. Donald J. Love
Richard L. & Clarissa S. Lovegrove
Mr. Euel L. Lovejoy
Edward F. & Sondra D. Lovell
Mr. Dixon D. Low
Ms. Frances C. Lowe
Mark S. & Wendy T. Lucas
Ms. Pamela T. Lucas
Ms. Geraldine L. Ludwick
George W. & M. Ann Luedke
Ms. Frances W. Lugar
Mr. James D. Lugar
Mrs. Gail Lumbert
Mr. Philip Lumbert
Mr. Clarence Lunsford
Ms. Susan F. Lynch
Ms. Virginia J. Lynch
Mr. Reynolds G. Lynch, Jr.
Mr. Reynolds G. Lynch III
Mr. & Mrs. Richard M. Lynn
Mr. Robert L. Lynn III
Robbie F. & Carolyn Lyon
Mr. Gregory L. Lyons
John C. & Roblyn G. Lystash
Mr. Granger MacFarlane
Mr. Edward I. Machado
Jeff & Rebecca W. Mackey
Mr. G. Nelson Mackey, Jr.
W. W. & Ruth B. Macy
Mr. Thomas C. MacMichael
Monroe D. & Kathryn A. MacPherson
Mr. Don D. Magoon
Mr. & Mrs. William Mahone V
Ms. Grace B. Main
Mr. Scott H. Malbon
Miss Audrey B. Malcolm
Mr. Harold Malcolm
Mr. Robert B. Manetta
Charles F. & Wanda P. Manuel
Mr. John A. Marfleet
Mr. John Markey
Clifton H. & Inara Marshall
Thomas S. & Mary H. Marshall
Frank Marshall III & Patricia L. Marshall
Ms. Dorothy W. Martin
Ms. Elizabeth W. Martin
Eugene M. & Judith G. Martin
Ms. Joanne H. Martin
John A. & Joan A. Martin
Mr. John F. Martin
Mrs. Lucy E. Martin
Mr. Lynwood Martin
Ms. Nancy F. Martin
Richard E. & Joe Ann Martin
Robert P. & Cheryl W. Martin
Dr. & Mrs. William M. Martin
Mr. William R. Martin, Sr.
Mr. Alex L. Martin III
Mr. C. Hampton Martin III
Robert L. & Barbara B. Martinet
Ms. Mildred R. Masi

Ms. Emily W. Mason
Ms. Gaynor A. Mason
Ms. La Rue B. Mason
Ms. Sara S. Mason
Mr. Thomas B. Mason
Dr. Joseph J. Masters
Mr. R. Lee Mastin
Dr. John M. Mathis
Ms. Nelle T. Mattern
Mr. Max W. Matthews
Ms. Susan K. Matts
William M. & Esther F. Maxey
Mr. Clarence W. May, Jr.
Mr. Darrell V. Maynard
Mr. Frank B. Mayorshi
Ms. Amanda B. McBreen
Ms. June McGraw McBroom
Mrs. Katherine M. McCain
Thomas S. & Phyllis K. McCallie
Ms. Irma C. McCarthy
Michael A. & Janice D. McCarthy
Mr. Kerry W. McCarty
Ms. Amanda B. McCaskill
Al & Betsy B. McClearn
Mr. G. Alan McClellan
Ms. Lorrie McCloskey
Mrs. Ora Belle McColman
Maston R. McCorkle, Jr. & Dorothy M.
    McCorkle
Mr. Robert W. McCown
Robert W. & Emily H. McCown
Ms. Brenda L. McDaniel
Ms. Jane N. McDaniel
Mrs. Katharine B. McDowell
Mr. Michael F. McFadden
Sam H. McGhee III & Sara L. McGhee
Dr. William F. McGuire
Kenneth G. & Shirley B. McLain
Mr. George A. McLean, Jr.
Ms. Susan McLelland-Ware
Mr. Lee A. McLennan
Ms. Helen S. McLeod
Dennis J. & Natalie J. McMahon
Mr. & Mrs. Lewis B. McNeace
Mr. Samuel P. McNeil
Mr. Robert McNichols
Mr. Smyth M. Meador
J. Thomas Meadows, Jr. & Leigh Meadows
Mr. Richard L. Meagher
Morton L. & Jessalyn G. Meier
Mr. William S. Mercer
Ms. Helen C. Meredith
Mr. Lucius M. Merritt
Mark R. & Ardis S. Merritt
Ms. Sharon B. Merritt
Jeffrey G. & Suzanne M. Messinger
Dr. Julien H. Meyer
Michael B. & Voleta L. Meyer
Dr. Julien H. Meyer, Jr.
Norwood C. & Lucille H. Middleton
Mr. & Mrs. G. A. Milan
Frank C. & Thelma P. Miller
Ms. Hilda D. Miller
John H. & Ethel M. Miller
Mr. & Mrs. T. Dalton Miller
Dr. Thomas K. Miller

Leslie H. Miller, Jr. & Jennifer S. Miller
Ms. Susan P. Millinger
Mr. Michael E. Mills
Curtis E. Mills, Jr. & Donna H. Mills
Ms. Margaret C. Milona
Dr. David P. Minichan, Jr.
Ms. Josephine B. Minnix
A. H. & Margery M. Minor
Ms. Donna L. Mitchell
Joe B. & Martha R. Mitchell
Mr. & Mrs. Marvin L. Mitchell
Mr. W. B. Mitchell
Ms. Zane R. Mizell
Dr. & Mrs. William M. Moir
Jim & Bonnie Molinary
James B. & Sara E. Monar
Mrs. Virginia Montague
Miss Lorana T. Moomaw
Mr. Ted Moomaw, Jr.
George W. & Susan S. Moore
Jack A. & Nancy S. Moore
Mrs. Jean T. Moore
Ms. Mae Moore
Mr. Mark H. Moore
Mrs. Mary P. Moore
Dr. Michael J. Moore
Ms. Sandra L. Moore
T. Christopher & Forrest D. Moore
Wilson P. & Wendy W. Moore
Ms. Ann J. Morgan
Mrs. E. B. Morgan
Dr. James K. Morgan
Dr. John E. Morgan
Ms. Shawn L. Morgan
Barton W. & Margaret J. Morris
John E. & Marie P. Morris
Ms. Judy Y. Morris
Ms. Margaret C. Morris
Gary & Robin Morse
Mrs. Doyne B. Moses
Mrs. Mary B. Moses
Mr. William S. Moses
Dr. & Mrs. Joseph T. Moskal
Mr. & Mrs. Kenneth L. Motley
Ms. Frances M. Mounfield
James C., Cecil J. & Polly Moynihan
Louis J. & Eva S. Mullineaux
Ms. Dorothy A. Mundy
Mr. G. Marshall Mundy
H. Robert & Mary P. Mundy
Mr. William K. Munzing
Fred R. & Helen M. Murko
Mrs. Nellie A. Murphy
W. E. & M. T. Murphy
Ms. Dorothy G. Murray
Edward R. & Linda J. Murray
Robert L. & Marjorie J. Murray
Alfred P. & Maureen M. Musci
Leonard A. & Elizabeth H. Muse
Ms. Lorraine T. Muse
Dr. Donna C. Musgrave
Ms. Reba J. Musselman
Mr. Howard E. Musser
John W. & Charlotte S. Myers
Mr. Daniel C. Naff, Jr.
Wesley W. Naff, Jr. & Angelia H. Naff

Mr. Michael J. Nagy
Ernest E. & Frances M. Nairne
Dr. Michael P. Najarian
David M. & Linda J. Nance
William A. & Clara J. Nash
Mr. Robert Natt
A. Carl Nave III & Tomi P. Nave
Mr. Robert F. Nay
Ms. Kelleigh A. Neal
Austin R. Neal, Jr. & Elizabeth S. Neal
William D. & Cheryle C. Neeley
Mrs. Jewell N. Neff
Mr. William J. Nelson, Jr.
George W. & Janet O. Nester
Mr. John Nettles
Mr. Arthur E. Neubauer
A. Jackson Newcomb, Jr. & Manette S.
    Newcomb
James B. & Dorothy H. Newman
Wayne C. & Barbara A. Newman
Louis M. & Sibyl W. Newton
Ms. Estelle Nichols
Mr. Edward H. Nicholson
Ms. Alicia Nickens
Mr. Harry C. Nickens
Lee M. & Lynn G. Noel
Charles S. & Elaine A. Noell
Mr. Winfred D. Noell
Mr. & Mrs. Robert L. Noell, Jr.
Mr. Lester Nolan
E. B. Noland, Jr. & Carolyn M. Noland
Mr. Keith Nonnenmacher
Dr. Randy J. Norbo
Ms. Winnie C. Norfleet
John & Carolina Norman
L. Elwood & Doris E. Norris
Dr. W. T. Norris, Jr.
Mr. C. A. Nottingham
Mr. P. A. Nunley
Ms. Jane M. O'Brien
George E. & Louise T. O'Hara
Ms. Martha G. O'Neill
Sam G. Oakey III & Elizabeth B. Oakey
James W. & Mary Obenshain
Mrs. Mary B. Olewiler
Mr. James R. Olin
David L. & Lisa P. Oliver
Frank L. & Frances L. Oliver
Ms. Mildred Orrick
Howard T. Orville, Jr. & Mary N. Orville
Mr. J. Lee E. Osborne
Mr. Woodrow W. Osborne
Mr. Charles H. Osterhoudt
Mrs. Walter Otey
Mr. & Mrs. F. W. Overstreet
Ms. Wanda E. Overstreet
Phil & Susan Owenby & Family
Mr. James M. Owens
Mr. E. C. Pace III
Steve & Kim Padgett
Robert D. & Jenny L. Painter
Ms. Dorothy H. Palmer
Ms. Carol B. Parker
William L. & Elizabeth R. Parker
Mr. Edward C. Parks
R. D. & Sharyn F. Parks

Mrs. Brooke M. Parrott
Mr. John H. Parrott
Mr. John H. Parrott, Jr.
Mr. John C. Parrott II
Lee R. & Edith M. Parsons
Ms. Mary F. Parsons
Dr. William W. Pasley
Mr. Louis A. Patrick
Mr. S. Kime Patsel
Ms. Ann E. Patterson
Dr. George M. Patterson
Norman S. & Myra L. Patterson
Dr. A. M. Patterson, Jr. & Carolyn M.
    Patterson
Hon. Richard C. Pattisall
Larry W. & Donna M. Patton
Mrs. Charles S. Patton, Jr.
Kevin & Sherry Pearson
Mrs. Martha M. Peck
Mr. Robert F. Peck
Homer S. Peck, Jr. & Beatrice P. Peck
Ms. Jeanne Pedigo
Ms. Marjorie F. Pedigo
William H. & Dorothy G. Pedrick
Dr. Criss-Tenna Peery
Mr. David R. Peery
Mr. Lewis W. Peery
Mr. & Mrs. Richard F. Pence
John W. & Jill B. Pendleton
Wayne B & Kathi Pennington
Mr. Dallas A. Peoples, Sr.
Ms. Dee Perdue
Ms. Marilyn G. Perdue
Ms. Rebecca S. Perdue
Dr. Enrique Perez
Ms. Marjorie F. Perez
Mr. Frank N. Perkinson, Jr.
Charles F. & Lynne U. Perry
Mr. Matt Perry
Ms. Ila G. Peters
John A. & Mildred B. Peters
Dr. Norma J. Peters
Philip L. & Patricia M. Peters
Ira B. Peters, Jr. & Doris T. Peters
Mr. David K. Peterson
Dr. Charles H. Peterson, Jr.
Mark & Gayle Petrozino
Mr. W. H. Pettigrew
Mrs. Barbara M. Petty
Mrs. Roma Pevler
Mr. Russell Peyton
Ms. Geneva P. Peyton
John H. & Cynthia M. Phelps
Mr. Glenn S. Phillips
Freeman M. Phillips, Jr. & Mary Y. Phillips
C. F. Phillips II
Ms. Margaret J. Philpott
Ms. Mary C. Pickett
Mr. & Mrs. J. D. Piedmont
Ms. Kathleen S. Pitman
Mrs. Virginia B. Pittman
Mr. Joseph E. Pittman, Jr.
Mr. & Mrs. R. E. Plasters, Sr.
Ms. W. Hope Player
Frank J. & Saundria L. Plecity
Ronald L. & Deborah E. Poff

William B. & Magdalen A. Poff
Mr. William F. Polhamus
Steve K. & Marie T. Pontius
Mr. Robert C. Poole
Dr. Robert E. Pooley
Louis F. & Agness P. Popp
Frank D. Porter III & Beverly Porter
Mr. Bittle W. Porterfield III
Winsdon N. & Madeline S. Pound
Mrs. Barbara B. Powell
Douglas W. & Doris Anne C. Powell
Shirley O. Powell
William C. & Lois M. Powell
Mr. John R. Pratt
Mrs. Margaret W. Pratt
John C. & Margaret S. Price
John D. & Phyllis Price
Mr. & Mrs. Robert I. Price, Jr.
Dr. John W. Priddy
Alton B. & Nancy K. Prillaman
Mr. Eddie P. Prillaman
Robert A. & Carol W. Pruner
Mr. Lawrence E. Ptaschek
J. Tyler & Beverley W. Pugh
Mrs. Rachel P. Pugh
Ms. Bonnie Pulliam
Mr. Stephen H. Purves
Mrs. Marilyn M. Putnam
Henry B. & Mary A. Quekemeyer
Mr. Michael K. Quinn
Donald J. & Judi A. Race
Mr. Michael A. Ragone
Tom & Elberta Raisbeck
Mr. Bill L. Rakes
Mr. & Mrs. William R. Rakes
Ms. Sara G. Rakestraw
Harold T. & Valerie W. Ramey
Mr. Joe W. Ramsey
Michael L. & Katherine Ramsey
Larry T. & Kendra M. Rasche
Mr. & Mrs. Curtis L. Ratliff
Ms. Susan Reardon
Tim B. & Paula C. Reardon
Mr. Richard H. Redmon
Mr. Morris D. Reece
Mr. Donald E. Reed
J. P. & Muriel C. Reed
Jerry L. & Ingrid Reed
Mr. John M. Reed
Mr. David W. Reed, Jr.
Ms. Earline H. Reid
Gary B. & Susan H. Reid
Mr. LanVan N. Reid
Ms. Harriet Remaine
Mr. C. John Renick
James A. & Dorothy D. Reynolds
Dr. James D. Rice
Mr. & Mrs. James H. Rice
Robert S. & Linda W. Rice
Mr. Steve Rice
Mr. Steve C. Rice
Mr. & Mrs. H. J. Richards
Mrs. Barbara B. Richardson
John J. & Virginia T. Richardson
Leslie G. & Dorothy E. Richardson
Robert N. & Joel W. Richert

Ms. Doris B. Ricker
Dave & Laurel Riddle
Mr. Layne E. Ridenour
Minnis E. & Louise Ridenour
Mr. Richard A. Rife
Mr. & Mrs. Berkeley H. Riley
Dr. Louis P. Ripley
Matthew & Miriam Rittberg
John D. & Frances M. Robbins
Ms. Leona H. Robbins
Mr. T. E. Roberts
Mr. W. J. Roberts
Mrs. W. J. Roberts
Thomas W. Roberts, Jr. & Robin R. Roberts
Mr. Andrew L. Roberts III
Mr. James B. Robertson
Ms. Jean L. Robertson
Mrs. Randal M. Robertson
Ms. Susan M. Robertson
Thomas E. & Claire T. Robertson
Mr. Thomas L. Robertson
Thomas M. Robertson, Jr. & Margaret M.
   Robertson
Mr. W. H. Robinson
Martin L. & Sherry R. Robison
Dr. William H. & Margaret R. Robison
Mr. William F. Rock
John G. Rocovich, Jr. & Sue Ellen Rocovich
Alvin W. & Martha Rodeck
Frank H. & Elizabeth B. Rodeniser
Mr. & Mrs. Elmer O. Rodes, Jr.
Mr. Thomas W. Roe, Jr.
Frank W. Rogers III & Doris J. Rogers
Gerald W. & Eleanor R. Roller
Mr. Alan E. Ronk
Ms. Brenda J. Rorrer
Mr. E. W. Rose
Mr. F. Gray Rose III
R. L. & Eula L. Rosenberger
Stephen H. & Mary C. Rosenoff
John S. Ross, Jr. & R. D. Ross
Gen. W. B. Rosson
Robert F. & Dorothy H. Roth
Teddy R. & Elaine S. Rountree
John H. & Margaret O. Rowe
Ms. V. Ann Rozier
Mr. & Mrs. Gordon F. Ruble
John C. Rudd, Jr. & Lisa K. Rudd
Dr. Robert E. Rude
Ms. Jean E. Ruegg
Ms. Nancy Rumbley
Mr. Joseph P. Rushbrooke
Charles D. Russell, Jr. & Terri K. Russell
Mr. Thomas D. Rutherfoord
Mr. Walton I. Rutherfoord
Ms. Gwen C. Rutherford
William B. Rutherford, Jr. & Ann S.
   Rutherford
Mr. James H. Ryals
Mr. Jack Sale
Mr. Nabil A. Samaha
Ms. Jennifer R. Sampson
John S. & Bettie R. Samuel
Jeffry L. & Susan L. Sanders
Mr. & Mrs. William M. Sanders
Raymond T. & Zona G. Sanford

Ms. Margaret M. Sarsfield
Mr. Patrick D. Sarsfield
V. J. & K. M. Sartini
Ms. Edith M. Sarver
Patton B. & Susan M. Saul
Mr. David Saunders
Frank W. & Agnes K. Saunders
Morris R. & Ina H. Saunders
Robert C. & Patricia M. Saunders
Ms. Virginia Moomaw Savage
Ltc. Joseph E. Scanlin
Ms. Elizabeth A. Schell
Robert C. & Margaret S. Schenk
Charles J. & Lynn F. Schleupner
Ms. Iris L. Schoenfield
Mr. & Mrs. Richard Schwarzwalder
Mr. Henry D. Scoggins
Ms. Evelyn Q. Scott
Mr. Gary W. Scott
Ms. Phyllis W. Scott
L. Paul Scott, Jr. & Cora C. Scott
Geoffrey L. & Nancy H. Seamans
James C. & Wanda P. Sears
Mr. J. M. Sears, Jr.
William T. & Audrey R. Self
Ms. Betsy Settles
Mr. Sylvan J. Sewell
Ms. Kathy M. Seymore
Mrs. Horace W. Seymour, Jr.
Mr. G. Scott Shackelford
Dr. Lee W. Shaffer
Mrs. Katherine D. Shank
Ms. Mary P. Shank
Mr. Patrick N. Shank
Ms. Ann M. Shannon
John S. & Elizabeth H. Shannon
Joel H. & Norma Shapiro
Manis & Violet Shapiro
Mr. Gregory H. Sharp
James K. & Wanda F. Sharp
Mr. Winston S. Sharpley
Donald F. & Barbara B. Sharrer
Dr. W. A. Shaver
L. Bruce & Connie P. Shaw
Mr. Richard E. Shawn
Mrs. W. N. Shearer
Thomas H. & Karen H. Shelton
Ms. Virginia Shepherd-Agee
Walter H. Shepherd III & Ruby K. Shepherd
Mr. Carl B. Sherertz
Mr. Robert F. Sherertz
Mr. Jack T. Sherman
Dr. Philip T. Shiner
Ralph D. & Harriette H. Shivers
Mr. Paul B. Shores, Jr.
Mr. Louis R. Showalter, Jr.
Ms. Joan H. Shrader
Ms. Madalon Shrader
William R. Shrader, Jr. & Shirley L. Shrader
Ms. Jacqueline Shuck
Edwin A. & Lois A. Sieveking
Mr. Barry Simmerman
Frank D. & Marian P. Simmons
Mr. Allen M. Simpson
Ms. Sharon K. Simpson
Dr. Lewis J. Singer

B. W. & Margaret H. Sink
Mr. W. H. Sisson
G. W. Skaggs, Jr. & Guelda T. Skaggs
Mrs. E. G. Skeens
Martin O. & Kelley Vest Skelly
Thomas W. & Dolores Skelly
J. Hampson & Judith B. Skinker
Ms. Mary E. Skinner
Dr. Arthur R. Slaughter
Michael J. & Annette L. Slenski
Ms. Elizabeth M. Slusher
Thomas H. & Gene H. Smallwood
Mrs. Mary Linda M. Smiley
Ms. Aileen G. Smith
David R. & Doreen E. Smith
Mr. & Mrs. Donald G. Smith
Mr. Edward M. Smith
Ms. Elizabeth Smith
Mr. Garnett E. Smith
Ms. Harriet H. Smith
Ms. Katherine S. Smith
Mr. Marshall N. Smith
Ms. Mary Ellen H. Smith
Ms. Neva J. Smith
Mr. Stuart F. Smith
Mr. T. Michael Smith
Ms. Valydia C. Smith
Ms. Virginia D. Smith
W. Ware & Elizabeth B. Smith
W. Ware Smith, Jr. & Isabella W. Smith
Ms. Marjorie S. Smithey
Raymond D. Smoot, Jr. & Joyce G. Smoot
Dr. James G. Snead
William C. & Jeanne B. Snead
James G. Snead, Jr. & Sandra O. Snead
David L. & Carol R. Snider
Ms. Judie S. Snipes
Mr. Lucas Snipes
Mrs. Georgia A. Snyder-Falkinham
Ms. Lydia E. Sochor
Ms. Mary H. Sochor
Alan G. & Lisa B. Soltis
Ms. Katherine T. Soniat
Mr. Eric P. Sorensen
Mrs. Eloise D. Sowder
Mr. William A. Sowers
Mr. & Mrs. Phillip F. Sparks
William F. & Karen Spears
Donna & Kelly Speas
Andrew E. & Diana G. Spencer
Warwick F. M. & Sarah J. Spencer
Bert & Clarine D. Spetzler
Ms. Katherine R. Spicer
Mrs. Robert J. Spiers
Ms. S. Ann Splitstone
Ms. Mary C. Spradlin
Ms. Ruth S. Spradlin
Ms. Margaret J. Springer
Dr. G. Sprinkle III
Mr. W. Earle Spruill, Jr.
Ms. Margaret St. Clair
Mr. Barry K. Stacy
Mr. Donald E. Stafford
Ms. Jan S. Stamper
Ms. Betty B. Stanley
Leonard P. & Elizabeth H. Stann

E. Duward & Helen H. Starkey
John W. & Lynda S. Starr
Dr. Anthony Stavola
Mrs. Marzetta W. Thomas
Charles H. & Frances S. Stebbins
Ms. Betty R. Steele
Mr. Robert E. Steele
W. Graham & Thelma L. Stephens
Bryan & Lynn M. Stephenson
Ms. Minnie P. Stevens
Philip S. Stevens, Jr. & Gale H. Stevens
Mr. & Mrs. Carson P. Stiff, Jr.
Carson P. Stiff, Sr. & Nelda G. Stiff
Miss Julie L. Stiff
Mr. Lewis A. Stinnett
Ms. Rebecca A. Stinnett
Mr. Edward F. Stinson
Mr. Bruce Stockburger
Mrs. Barbara A. Stockstill
Kurt R. & Laura S. Stockstill
Thomas J. & Michelle A. Stoecker
Mrs. Harriett M. Stokes
Mrs. Anne M. Stone
Ms. Elizabeth Stone
Mr. F. Anderson Stone
Dr. & Mrs. W. Conrad Stone
Robert S. & Patricia K. Stratton
Mr. M. L. Strauss
Ms. Doris J. Strickland
Ms. Gloria Strickland
Mr. L. Douglas Strickland
Gene P. & Linda P. Stuckey
Clyde R. & Helen Stultz
Mrs. Florence C. Stump
Dr. Herbert F. Sudranski
Ms. Ceara O. Sullivan
Ms. Bertha Y. Sumpter
Joseph L. & Kathleen S. Surace
Mr. J. H. Surkamer, Jr.
Mr. & Mrs. Lee I. Sutphin, Jr.
Mrs. Emily M. Sutton
Mr. Donald M. Sutton, Sr.
Ray W. & Doris B. Swanson
Ms. Helen K. Sweeney
J. Brantley & Jane S. Sydnor
Mr. Robert Szathmary
Mr. & Mrs. E. C. Taliaferro
Ms. Betty C. Tanner
Mr. Ken S. Tanner
Mr. & Mrs. Nathan H. Tanner, Jr.
Mr. Cengiz Tanverdi
Ms. Marilyn K. Tarleton
Clayton J. & Betty G. Tate
Eugene G. & Gladys S. Tayloe
Mrs. Minnie B. Taylor
Rev. Noel C. Taylor
Ms. Victoria C. Taylor
T. Edward Taylor, Sr. & Shirley Taylor
Jefferson K. & Susan G. Teass
Ms. Sandra S. Teigland
Mr. Robert H. Teter
Ms. Judith K. Tewksbury
Mr. John B. Thacker
Ms. Sadie J. Tharp
Bruce R. & Nancye P. Thomas
Mr. Donald W. Thomas

Mrs. Douglas M. Thomas
Mrs. Marzetta W. Thomas
Ms. Melba B. Thomas
Mr. Quinn D. Thomas
Mr. & Mrs. Victor A. Thomas
Dr. William O. Thomas
Raymond C. Thomas, Jr. & Rosemary H.
   Thomas
Dale A. & Mary Jo Z. Thompson
Mr. Edward Thompson
Robert P. & Nell C. Thompson
William C. & Ellen L. Thomsen
Ms. Pamela J. Thomson
Hugh A. & Laura A. Thornhill
Mr. Andrew C. Thornton III
Mr. James R. Thorpe
Mr. John L. Thorsten
Ms. Judy R. Thornton
Ms. Pamelia Tiernan-Smith
Dr. Jonathan S. Till
Robert E. Tonkinson, Jr. & Cameo B.
   Tonkinson
A. James & Harriet E. Travitz
Mr. Glover M. Trent
Mr. Eric Trethewey
Mrs. Miriam K. Trimble
David & Ann Trinkle
Mr. William F. Trinkle
Ms. Virginia C. Trippeer
Ms. Anne H. Trout
Mr. Charles S. Tubman
Dr. Kenneth D. Tuck
Dr. F. Lee Tucker
Ms. Alice C. Tuckwiller
Mrs. Kathryn C. Tully
Mr. John R. Turbyfill
Mr. Fancher T. Turner
Mark C. & Gayle N. Turner
Mr. & Mrs. A. L. Turner, Jr.
Mrs. Nancy E. Rankin Tyler
Ms. Evelyn S. Tyree
Paul & Zosia Umbarger
Mrs. W. A. Umberger
Richard A. & Gail M. Ungerer
Mr. & Mrs. John H. Urquhart
Ms. Kimberly M. Usler
Mrs. Annabelle Vaden
Miss Mary Jane Vaden
Mr. Charles C. Vail, Jr.
Ms. Kathleen Van Buren
Ms. Phyllis W. Van Eps
Ms. Linda R. Van Luik
Dr. Samuel F. Vance III
Karl A. & Paula J. Vandegriff
Jack & Nell W. Varner
John W. & Audrey H. Vaughan
Ms. Stephanie C. Vaughan
Mr. Joe H. Vaughn, Jr.
Dr. Robert L. Vermillion
Ms. Lynn W. Via
Ms. Sarah R. Viar
Mr. Claiborne W. Vinyard
Mr. & Mrs. Darnall Vinyard
Ms. Ernestine M. Vinyard
Mr. J. H. Vipperman
Mr. Anthony C. Wade

Ben F. & Janice W. Wade
Ms. Evelyn C. Wade
Jimmie L. & Ellen V. Wade
Robert C. & Susan B. Wagner
R. A. & Meredith B. Waid
Mr. James G. Wajciechowski
Mr. Jack L. Wakeland
Mr. Gary M. Waldo
Mrs. O. L. Waldron
Mrs. A. Waldrop
Dr. John T. Walke
Mr. Eugene R. Walker
Mrs. John L. Walker
Mr. John W. Walker
Ms. Marie T. Walker
Dr. Rome H. Walker
George H. & Billie O. Wall
Ms. Jean O. Wallace
Ms. Katherine O. Wallace
Ms. Miriam Wallace
William P. Wallace, Jr. & Jane I. Wallace
Dr. Peter A. Wallenborn, Jr.
Dr. David C. Walton
Ms. Sarah G. Walton
Wylie E. & Diane Walton
Mr. W. H. Walton, Jr.
Mr. Lilburn E. Ward III
Ms. Betty G. Ware
Mr. Michael E. Warner
Thomas N. & Jean D. Warren
Mr. Charles E. Warsaw II
Norman C. & Bertha S. Washer
Mr. Carlton B. Waskey
Mr. Douglas C. Waters
Ms. Marjorie F. Waters
Mrs. Mary S. Watkins
Ms. Ethel P. Watson
Mr. William C. Watson
E. Mark & Deborah L. Watts
Mrs. Louise P. Watts
Mr. & Mrs. William Watts
E. Wilson Watts, Jr. & Barbara A. Watts
Ms. Laura S. Weaver
Ms. Margaret L. Weaver
Ronald S. & Janice C. Weaver
Mr. Stephen E. Weaver
Mr. Barry C. Webb
Dr. Jesse Webster
Mr. John R. A. Webster
Clifford R. & Ginger Weckstein
Norbert L. & Gloria B. Weckstein
Clarence O. & Mildred L. Wegmann
Ms. Nora Weikel
William F. & Ruth K. Weller
Mr. N. W. Wellford, Jr.
Ms. Mary C. Wellington Hunt
D. Christopher & Eleanor B. Wells
Hugh H. & Peggy H. Wells
Mr. Jeffrey R. Wendell
Dr. Jane Wentworth
L. J. & Agnes Wertz
Richard W. & Jean U. Wertz
Mr. Lewis E. Wertz, Sr.
Mr. Stephen N. Wesby
Ms. Lucy A. Wharton
Mitch V. & Julie H. Wheeler

Ms. Shirley Wheeler
James E. Wheless, Jr. & Carolyn L. Wheless
Ms. Jean B. Whitaker
Mr. James A. White
Dr. Paul F. White
Robert M. & Carol C. White
Ms. Virginia C. White
William G. & Linda J. White
Laurence A. White, Jr. & Earlene S. White
William White, Sr. & Joyce White
Ms. Dorothy C. Whitehead
Ms. Ann R. Whitenack
Mr. & Mrs. J. W. Whitenack
Ms. Linda Whitenack
Mr. Vance Whitfield
Ms. Sarah C. Whiting
Ms. Amy Whitlow
Ms. Anne B. Whitlow
Ms. Sue Whitlow
Dr. William R. Whitman, Jr.
Mr. & Mrs. Glenn R. Whitmer
Richard S. Whitney, Jr. & Carole S. Whitney
Frederick A. & Elizabeth S. Whittaker
Mr. & Mrs. F. H. Wilbourne
Roger P. & Sheila L. Wiley
Ms. Terra L. Wiley
Ms. Virginia Moore Wiley
Ms. Teresa J. Wilhelm
Dr. A. J. Jackie Wilkerson
John W. & Margaret W. Wilks
Mr. Forrest S. Williams
G. Earl & Leatha O. Williams
Mr. Goldie Beckett Williams
Mr. Richard L. Williams
Robert L. & Anne Williams
Samuel J. & Elizabeth Williams
Mr. & Mrs. Cranston Williams, Jr.
Mr. Jerry T. Williams, Jr.
Edwin L. Williams II & Jean B. Williams
Ms. Karen L. Williamson
Luther L. & Zelma H. Williamson
Ms. Ruth W. Williamson
Mrs. Marguerite S. Willis
Robert A. & Karen E. Willis
Sidney H. & Karen C. Willis
Mrs. Holman Willis, Jr.
Mr. Robert E. Wills
Mr. Stephen L. Willson
Bayes E. & Ella W. Wilson
Edwin M. & June M. Wilson
James C. & Betty R. Wilson
Ms. Judy T. Wilson
Ms. Laura B. Wilson
Thomas E. & Beth Wilson
Dr. James T. Wilson III
Mr. Richard P. Wimberley
Ms. Betty C. Winfree
Dr. Thomas M. Winn, Jr.
Robert R. & Helen J. Winters
Matthew M. & Nancy W. Wise
Michael & Danielle Wise
Brian & Andrea Wishneff
Mr. Albert A. Witcher
Donald R. & Ellen M. Witt
Ms. Linda Witt
Charles D. & Betty A. Wohlford

Mrs. S. L. Wohlford
Dr. Barry Wolfe
Ms. Kitty Womack
Mr. Paul J. Woo, Jr.
Bruce M. & Jennifer M. Wood
Ms. Catherine A. Wood
Mr. Stephen T. Wood, Jr.
Mr. M. Eugene Wood III
Thomas G. & Melissa D. Woodford
James M. Woodruff, Jr. & Elizabeth R. Woodruff
Mr. M. Lanier Woodrum
Ms. Meredith M. Woodrum
Clifton A. Woodrum III & Emily A. Woodrum
Mr. & Mrs. James P. Woods, Jr.
J. Randy & Karen Woodson
Ms. Jo Lynn D. Woody
Ms. Linda Price Woody
Oliver S. & Reese W. Woody
Mr. & Mrs. Robert W. Woody
Mr. O. Sands Woody, Jr.
Daniel E. & Nancy C. Wooldridge
Mr. & Mrs. S. K. Woosley
Ms. Victoria H. Worrell
Goodrich & Julia Wright
Mr. & Mrs. Joseph B. Wright
Ms. Kathleen M. Wright
Mr. Kenneth L. Wright
Mr. Phillip P. Wright
Roland G. & Merle P. Wright
Ms. Suzanne R. Wright
Mrs. Charles A. Wright, Jr.
J. L. & Lena M. Wyatt
Ms. Sandra M. Wyatt
Mrs. Eda W. Wynn
Ms. Janet E. Wynot
Ms. Gladys L. Yates
Dr. Harry R. Yates, Jr.
Mr. Harold Yeglin
D. Jack & Margaret B. Young
Mr. Donnovan Young
Ms. Helen E. Young
Mr. James M. Young
Ms. Melissa Amos Young
Roger D. & Cecil D. Young
Ms. Lavinia Zerbee
Mr. Howard C. Zerbst
Mr. David Zimmerman & Ms. Carolyn Harrison
Charles & Lois T. Zmitrovis

PHOTO CREDITS

Roanoke Valley History Museum – Cover; title page; 12 bottom left; 17 top; 30; 37 top; 38 top and bottom left; 47; 61 right; 62; 86; 90

Special Collections, Newman Library, Virginia Tech – 18 top left; 20 top right and bottom; 21; 25; 27; 29; 37 bottom; 41 top right; 45; 46; 52; 54; 57 bottom left; 58 top left; 61 bottom left; 63 top; 64; 69; 75 bottom; 81 bottom; 92; 94; 97

Norfolk and Western Railway Photo Collection of Kenneth L. Miller – 3; 7; 9; 14 left and top right; 16; 17 bottom left, bottom right; 18 bottom left, top right; 20 top left; 32; 38 bottom right; 39; 41 top and bottom left, bottom right; 42; 51; 55; 57 top, bottom right; 58 top right, bottom; 59; 63 bottom; 66; 71; 88

Roanoke Times & World News – 12 top; 50; 72 top right; 75 left; 79; 85; 102; 103; 104; 108; 110

Roanoke Regional Chamber of Commerce – 61 top left; 72 top left, bottom; 76.

Norfolk Southern Corporation – 10; 12 bottom right; 82.

Moore's – 67

John Lambert Associates – 75 top right

Virginia Tech Photo Services – 98

Muncy Fine Photography – Endpapers; 22; 24 top left; 34; 48; 49; 73

Individuals – 5 Dorothy Piedmont; 24 Eric Fitzpatrick; 31 Henry Hewitt; 44, 53 Warren Webb; 80 Joe Corne; 81 Betty Nappier; 87 Janet Jenkins.

COLOR PLATES

Plate 1 – left, bottom right, John Lambert Associates; top right, bottom, Roanoke Valley Convention and Tourist Bureau

Plates 2 and 3 – Roanoke Valley History Museum

Plate 4 – left, John Lambert Associates; top and bottom right, Roanoke Valley Convention and Tourist Bureau

Plate 5 – John Lambert Associates

Plate 6 – John Lambert Associates

Plate 7 – John Lambert Associates

Plate 8 – Norfolk Southern Corporation

Plate 9 – Norfolk Southern Corporation

Plate 10 – Roanoke Times & World News

Plate 11 – Roanoke Times & World News

Plate 12 – John Lambert Associates